FOCUS ON
BRITAIN TODAY

Clare Lavery

MACMILLAN
PUBLISHERS

First published 1993

Published by MACMILLAN PUBLISHERS LIMITED
London and Basingstoke

Illustrations by Art Construction

Produced by AMR Ltd

A CIP catalogue record for this book is available from the British Library.

ISBN 0-333-56669 6

Printed in Spain

Contents

Acknowledgements

Invaders and visitors

Who are the British?

George Michael's real name is Giorgious Panayiotou. His family emigrated to Britain from Cyprus. There are 200,000 Cypriots living in Britain today, most of whom settled in North London.

Frank Bruno was born in London in 1961. His father was from Dominica and his mother from Jamaica. In 1985 he became the European heavyweight boxing champion.

Diane Abbott is a Member of Parliament. She is well-known throughout Britain because she was the first black woman ever to be elected to the British parliament. Her parents emigrated to Britain from Jamaica in the 1950s.

Maria Gomez was born in London in 1980. Her father comes from Gran Canaria. Maria's mother was born in London but her family originate from Russia and Poland. They came to Britain at the beginning of the twentieth century. Maria is bilingual Spanish-English.

Pre-reading

1 Match these words with their definitions.

originate from   to make a place your home

emigrate   to come from (the place where your ancestors once lived)

settle   to change countries / move to another country

2 Write a short paragraph about yourself. Use the texts above and these questions to help you.

Where were you born?

Where did your family originally come from?

Did your ancestors emigrate?

When did your family settle in your town?

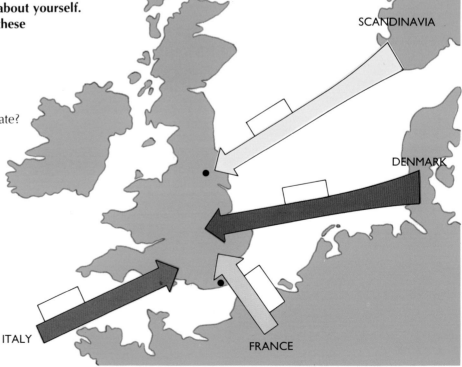

Key

- Romans
- Vikings
- Angles, Saxons, Jutes
- Normans

SCANDINAVIA

DENMARK

ITALY

FRANCE

Historical Invasions

Who were the invaders? When did they come?

Since the 1960s Britain has often been described as a 'multicultural society', which means that it is made up of a variety of cultures and peoples. Firstly, Britain consists of four countries: England, Scotland, Wales and Northern Ireland. Each has its own customs and traditions and, in the case of Scotland, even a different education system and different laws.

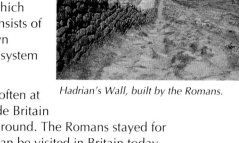
Hadrian's Wall, built by the Romans.

The first inhabitants were Iberians and Celts who settled on the land and were often at war with each other. In AD 43 the Roman Emperor Claudius invaded, and made Britain a Roman province. Julius Caesar had previously visited Britain to have a look around. The Romans stayed for three hundred years, and built villas, roads and towns. Many Roman remains can be visited in Britain today. Later, Christian missionaries came from other parts of the Roman Empire to bring Christianity to the people.

The Romans finally abandoned Britain in AD 410 and a long period of invasions by Nordic peoples (from northern Germany and Scandinavia) started. The Angles, Saxons and Jutes began to settle from the sixth to the eighth centuries, and the Angles gave England its name. These invaders introduced a new culture to Britain, and even today British customs and habits are described as 'Anglo-Saxon'. Anglo-Saxon England was one of the most civilised countries in Europe, with organised systems of agriculture and trade. The Vikings came from Scandinavia in the tenth century; they settled in the north and made the town of York the capital of their kingdom.

The last successful invasion of Britain was in 1066, which is an important date in history books in British schools. Duke William of Normandy (William the Conqueror) defeated the English at the Battle of Hastings (in the south of England), and the Normans and the French settled in Britain over the next three centuries. French became the language of the nobility (the King and the aristocrats) and, with Latin, the language of the legal system and of government.

Reading activity

3 **a** Read the text and write the correct century in each of the boxes on the map.
   b Write the names of the two towns mentioned in the correct places on the map.

4 Who came first? Put the invaders in the correct order.

Vikings   Saxons   Celts

Romans   Normans

1st   _____
2nd   _____
3rd   _____
4th   _____
5th   _____

5 Write these numbers from the text in words.

1960s   _____

300   _____

8th   _____

1066   _____

The British Empire
Britain invades other countries
Pre-reading

1 **Look at the list of ex-British colonies in the box. Can you label them on the map? The first one is done for you.**

Jamaica	Guyana	Australia	New Zealand	Sierra Leone	Gold Coast (Ghana)
South Africa	Cameroon	Egypt	Ceylon (Sri Lanka)	Tasmania	Malaya (Malaysia)
Borneo (Kalimantan)	The Gambia				

Check your answers with an atlas or with your teacher.

2 **Read and answer.**

Why did the British want an Empire?
How big was the Empire?
Why was India important to Britain?

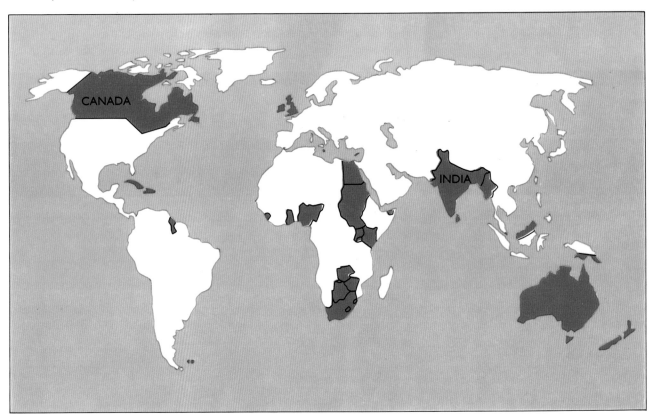

KEY WORDS
colonies
continent
British Empire

During the nineteenth century, Britain built up an empire of **colonies** which stretched into every **continent**. There were colonies or settlements in China, India, Africa, South America, the West Indies (the Caribbean), Canada and Australasia. Maps of the world used the colour red to show the countries which were part of the **British Empire**, and by 1914 a quarter of the countries in the world were coloured red on the maps! It was said that the sun never set on the British Empire, because at any time of day the sun was always shining on a British colony somewhere in the world.

3 **Before you read on, answer these questions.**

a Which continent is your country in?

b Has your country ever had colonies or an empire?

KEY WORDS	**EXPLORATION AND TRADE**
explorers	British **explorers** started sailing the world in the sixteenth century, when Elizabeth the First was queen of England. The explorers went in search of new lands and new sources
raw material	of **raw material**.
Australia	**Australia** was discovered by Captain Cook, a British explorer, and was first used as a prison – criminals were sent to the new colony from Britain as a severe punishment.
missionaries	British explorers and **missionaries** opened up the route to **Africa**. Africa became very
Africa	important for European and American merchants who bought and sold Africans as
slaves	**slaves**. These slaves were shipped to the West Indies and North America to work on sugar, cotton and tobacco plantations. The cotton, sugar and tobacco were traded in London, and today London remains one of the world's most important centres for trading
commodities	**commodities**. The profits of the slave trade were invested in banks and in industry, and were used to build railway and other transport systems in Britain. The trade from its
industrial development	colonies provided money for **industrial development**, and as Britain became richer and more powerful it was able to add to their number.

4 **Before you read on, answer these questions.**

  a Captain Cook was an explorer. Can you name any other explorers?
  b Bananas do not grow in Britain. Can you name two raw materials that your country needs to buy from another country?

KEY WORDS	**THE JEWEL IN THE CROWN**
sea route	Ever since explorers and seamen discovered a **sea route** to India, Europeans (including the Dutch, the French and the Portuguese) wanted to trade there. India was a rich source of raw materials such as spices, diamonds, rubber, tea and coffee. Britain could
trade	also sell manufactured products to India, and so profits from **trade** with India were very important for Britain's industrial development in the nineteenth century. Britain wanted India for itself, and called it the 'Jewel in the Crown', in other words, the most precious
ships	possession in the Empire. British **ships** controlled the sea route to India, and countries on
Suez Canal	the route were carefully watched. This is why places such as South Africa and the **Suez Canal** (in Egypt) were important to the British. Britain needed to control these places to keep the route to India safe, and so protect trade. When you visit India today, you will constantly be reminded of its past British connection. If you drink a cup of tea in England, think of the efforts that the British made to protect the tea route! Finally, you will now understand why many British schools serve Indian food in the canteen at lunchtime, because a big empire leads to an exchange of habits, customs and people.

Before you read on:-

There were two possible routes to India by sea from Britain. Mark these routes on the map of the Empire on page 4.

THE COMMONWEALTH

Today, almost all of the original countries of the Empire have gained their independence from Britain. Many agreed to stay together as a 'family', in a union of countries called the Commonwealth. They share a history, the English language, common traditions, and cultural and sporting ties.

Ethnic minorities in the UK

A

B

Pre-reading

1 a When and where do you think each of the two illustrations is located?

b Look at A. Why do you think this British family were living in India? What was the man's job? What type of lifestyle did the family have?

c Look at photo B. Why do you think this family have decided to live in Britain? Can you think of any problems for immigrants arriving in a new country (e.g. not knowing the language)?

Reading

KEY WORDS	A CHANGING SOCIETY
	Why did immigrants come to Britain? **Where did they come from?**
migration persecution	There has always been a movement of people in and out of Britain. This is called **migration**. At the end of the nineteenth century and in the early years of the twentieth century about 100,000 Eastern European Jews arrived to escape from religious **persecution** in Russia and Poland. In the nineteenth century Britain received large numbers of Irish immigrants who came over to work on the rapidly expanding canal and railway networks or to escape from starvation caused by the failure of the potato crop.
recruiting labour shortage	After the Second World War, Britain started **recruiting** European workers to help rebuild its shattered economy. Some came from Poland and Italy and many from Ireland. All these new workers came to escape poverty in their own countries. However, the supply of European workers was insufficient to meet Britain's needs. In the 1950s and 1960s Britain needed workers in textile manufacture, heavy industry, transport and health services. The **labour shortage** was especially severe in areas of low-paid work such as cleaning, catering and transport.

Britain now looked to its colonies and former colonies in the **Commonwealth** for help. Between 1950 and 1961, **immigration** from the Caribbean and India was encouraged by British employers. These new immigrants had experience of British administration from the time when their countries were British colonies, and most of them spoke English as a first or second language. They looked forward to a better life for their children in the **'Mother Country'**. Unfortunately, they found a very different reality when they arrived in Britain. They had difficulty getting good jobs and housing because of the colour of their skin. Most jobs available to them were poorly paid and they had to work very long hours. It was, therefore, very difficult for them to respond when asked by hostile local people: 'Why did you come here?' In fact, Britain had colonised their countries and founded an empire before these new immigrants came to Britain. They were not prepared for the **racial discrimination** they experienced on arrival in their new home.

In 1971 the Commonwealth **Immigration Act** restricted the number of new immigrants, although an exception was made in 1972 when many thousands of Asians were expelled from Uganda (in East Africa) by General Idi Amin and most of them settled in Britain. The year 1971 was also significant as was the year when the United Kingdom became a member of the **EEC** (European Economic Community, also called the Common Market). The number of immigrants from other EEC countries more than doubled between 1974 and 1984, and is expected to increase throughout the 1990s. One particular aspect of international migration in recent years has been the increasing number of **refugees** who move to Britain for political freedom and safety (**asylum**). In the period from 1979-89, 34,000 people (mainly from Turkey, Somalia, Sri Lanka and Uganda), were allowed to stay in Britain as refugees.

Interpretation

2 Complete this table with information from the text.

Date	Country of origin	Reason for move to Britain
19th century	Russia	Religious persecution
	Poland	

3 **a** Have people ever emigrated to your country? When? Why?
   b Has a member of your family ever changed country?

4 Look at the diagram below and answer the questions:
   a List the countries of origin of Britain's overseas population, starting with the highest percentage.
   b In 1981, over 3 million people out of a total of 54 million were from overseas. If 43% were born in New Commonwealth countries, how many people does this percentage represent?

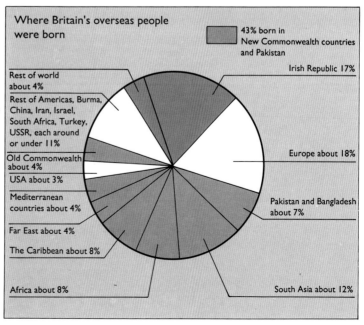

Where Britain's overseas people were born

- 43% born in New Commonwealth countries and Pakistan
- Irish Republic 17%
- Europe about 18%
- Pakistan and Bangladesh about 7%
- South Asia about 12%
- Africa about 8%
- The Caribbean about 8%
- Far East about 4%
- Mediterranean countries about 4%
- USA about 3%
- Old Commonwealth about 4%
- Rest of Americas, Burma, China, Iran, Israel, South Africa, Turkey, USSR, each around or under 11%
- Rest of world about 4%

Source: 1981 Census

7

CASE STUDY: West Indians and the British experience

Given their relationship to the British, the West Indians tended to think of themselves as British and the British encouraged them to do so. Like the British, they were Christians; they spoke English; their history was closely tied up with that of Britain; they learnt English nursery rhymes; they saluted the Union Jack before starting their classes in schools; they studied and took pride in British history; the three major counties in Jamaica were called Cornwall, Middlesex and Surrey; Trafalgar Square and Nelson's Column in Bridgetown, Barbados were much older than the ones in London; the King or Queen's Birthday and Empire Day were the most celebrated days of the year; they looked upon Britain as their mother country, and so on. No doubt the West Indians knew that they were of African descent and black in colour and therefore different from the British. However, they knew too that they were British in their political loyalties and that a large part of their culture was British...

The British in Britain saw them differently. To be sure, some of them did recognise the similarities in religion and language. For the bulk of British society, however, it was the colour of the West Indians that mattered more. They referred to them by negative labels such as 'niggers', resented their presence, and generally avoided them. The West Indians thought that they were black but British, and could not see why they could not be both. By contrast the British thought that they were black and *therefore not* British.

Text adapted from The Open University, E354, Block 3, Unit 10

Reading

1 Culture means a way of life/lifestyle. Read the text and find two cultural similarities between the West Indians and the British.

2 The text gives examples of some of the things which make up a culture, e.g.
Christians = religion = culture;
Nursery rhymes = traditional music = culture.

  a Find two other things in the text that could be described as part of a country's culture.

  b Working in pairs, make a list of examples of your culture, e.g.

  a type of food you cook for special occasions

  a national song

  a famous place or monument

  a dress or costume that you wear at festivals

  special words that are only used in your town or region

  Compare your list with the rest of the class.

  c Choose a country you know well or are interested in. Find out about the country. Make a list of all the things you associate with the culture of that country.

FACT FILE

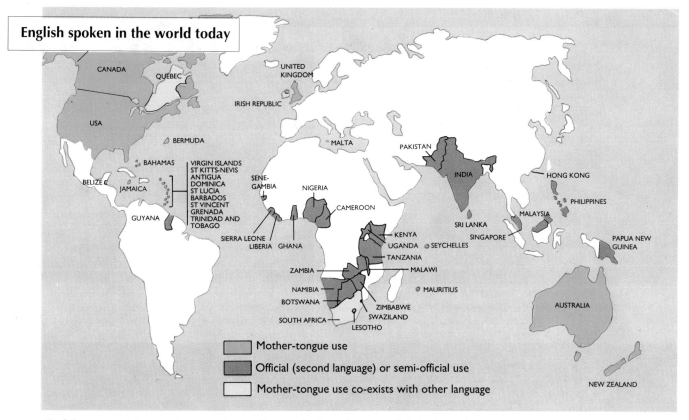

English spoken in the world today

CANADA
QUEBEC
UNITED KINGDOM
IRISH REPUBLIC
USA
BERMUDA
MALTA
PAKISTAN
BAHAMAS
VIRGIN ISLANDS
ST KITTS-NEVIS
ANTIGUA
DOMINICA
ST LUCIA
BARBADOS
ST VINCENT
GRENADA
TRINIDAD AND
TOBAGO
BELIZE
JAMAICA
SENE-GAMBIA
NIGERIA
CAMEROON
INDIA
HONG KONG
PHILIPPINES
MALAYSIA
GUYANA
SIERRA LEONE
LIBERIA
GHANA
KENYA
UGANDA
SEYCHELLES
TANZANIA
SRI LANKA
SINGAPORE
PAPUA NEW GUINEA
ZAMBIA
MALAWI
NAMIBIA
BOTSWANA
SOUTH AFRICA
ZIMBABWE
SWAZILAND
LESOTHO
MAURITIUS
AUSTRALIA
NEW ZEALAND

Mother-tongue use

Official (second language) or semi-official use

Mother-tongue use co-exists with other language

Find four countries on the map (apart from Britain) where English is the mother tongue.

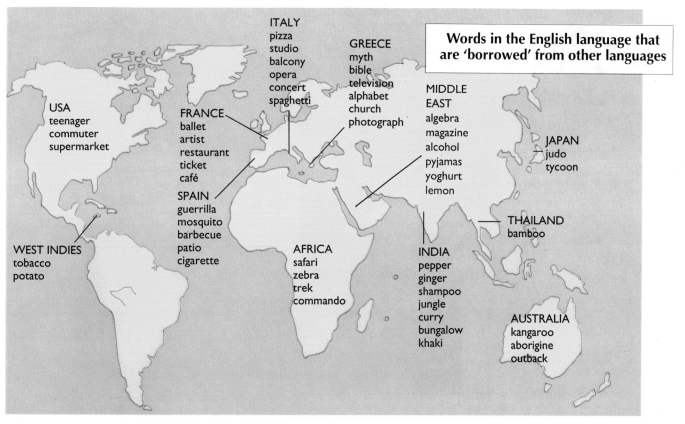

Words in the English language that are 'borrowed' from other languages

ITALY
pizza
studio
balcony
opera
concert
spaghetti

GREECE
myth
bible
television
alphabet
church
photograph

MIDDLE EAST
algebra
magazine
alcohol
pyjamas
yoghurt
lemon

USA
teenager
commuter
supermarket

FRANCE
ballet
artist
restaurant
ticket
café

JAPAN
judo
tycoon

SPAIN
guerrilla
mosquito
barbecue
patio
cigarette

THAILAND
bamboo

WEST INDIES
tobacco
potato

AFRICA
safari
zebra
trek
commando

INDIA
pepper
ginger
shampoo
jungle
curry
bungalow
khaki

AUSTRALIA
kangaroo
aborigine
outback

Make a list of any English words that are used in your country.

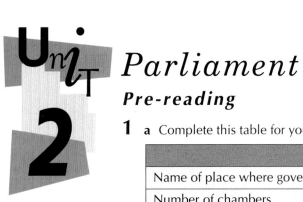

Parliament

Pre-reading

1 a Complete this table for your own country.

	YOUR COUNTRY	BRITAIN
Name of place where government meets		
Number of chambers		
Head of State		
Main political parties		

b Look up the meaning of 'Commons' and 'Lord' in a dictionary.

KEY WORDS	THE PALACE OF WESTMINSTER
	Britain is administered from the Palace of Westminster in London. This is also known as the Houses of Parliament. Parliament is made up of two chambers – the House of
Commons Lords elected inherited seat	**Commons** and the House of **Lords**. The members of the House of Lords are not **elected**; they qualify to sit in the House because they are bishops of the Church of England, aristocrats who have **inherited** their **'seats'** from their fathers, people with titles, or senior judges of the legal system. There has been talk of reform this century because many Britons think that this system is undemocratic.
Members of Parliament constituencies	The House of Commons, by contrast, has 651 seats which are occupied by **Members of Parliament (MPs)** who are elected by the British public. The United Kingdom is divided into **constituencies**, each of which has an elected MP in the House of Commons.
candidate votes	Each of the major political parties appoints a representative (**candidate**) to compete for each seat. Smaller parties may have a candidate in only a few constituencies. There may be five or more parties fighting for one seat, but only one person – the candidate who gets the greatest number of **votes** – can win. Some parties win a lot of seats and some win very few, or none at all.
	The Queen, who is the Head of State, opens and closes Parliament. All new laws are debated (discussed) by MPs in the Commons, then debated in the Lords, and finally signed by the Queen. All three are part of Parliament in Britain.

Reading comprehension

2 a What is the difference between the Commons and the Lords?
  b Why do some people think the House of Lords needs to be reformed?
  c What are the three main components of the British Parliament?
  d Which of the following people would not have a seat in the House of Lords?

All judges	Bishops	Policemen	MPs
Dukes	The Lord Chancellor		Nuns
Sons of life peers		Barons	

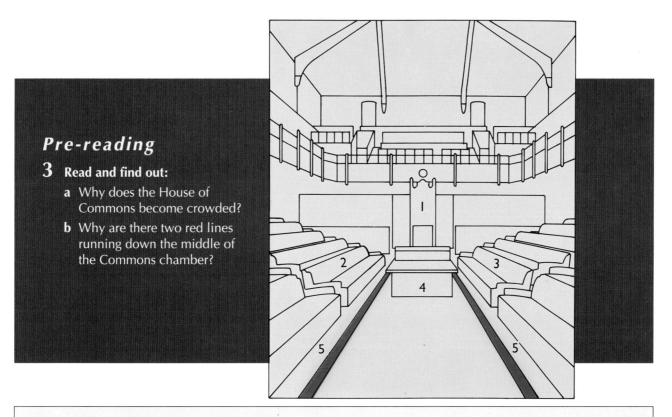

Pre-reading

3 Read and find out:

a Why does the House of Commons become crowded?

b Why are there two red lines running down the middle of the Commons chamber?

KEY WORDS	**THE HOUSE OF COMMONS**
	There are 651 MPs in Britain, but the Chamber of the House of Commons is quite small; it has seats for only 437, so when there is something important to discuss it can become very crowded and MPs squeeze on to the benches or sit on the steps. The House of Commons has a
Speaker	chairman, called the **Speaker**, whose job is to keep the House in order, a little like a referee at a football match. He or she shouts 'Order! Order!' when MPs start shouting at each other, or when the discussion gets out of control. The Speaker sits in the centre at the back, on a high
chair	**chair**, and can see the whole Chamber from this position. The office of Speaker is neutral, i.e. he or she is not a member of a political party.
red lines	There are **red lines** running along each side of the Chamber. This means that the Chamber is divided in two. Since Britain traditionally has two main political parties, the Conservative Party and the Labour Party, each party can have its own side! The party which is in government (i.e. has the most MPs elected) sits on the right. The two red lines on the floor must not be crossed, to prevent either side attacking the other during a debate. MPs in Britain do not normally use physical violence, but the red lines are a historical tradition; in the past, MPs used to carry swords into the Chamber and the distance between the two lines is too wide for a sword fight!
front benches	The most important MPs sit on the **front benches** and are therefore called frontbenchers. Younger and less experienced MPs sit on the back benches and are known as backbenchers.
Government Opposition table	The ministers of the **Government** sit on the front bench to the right, whilst the **Opposition** frontbenchers sit on the left. When the Prime Minister (the leader of the party in government) or any other leading politician makes a speech, they stand at the **table** in the centre, below the Speaker's chair. These seating arrangements have existed for hundreds of years.

Reading

4 Use the picture and text to identify the following:

The Opposition front bench	The Speaker's chair	The Table of the House
Red lines on the floor	The Government front bench	

Conclusion

5 Now complete the table in Exercise 1 for Britain. Use all the texts in this section to help you.

The greatest show on earth?

Pre-reading

1 **a** How often do you see your country's politicians on TV?

b Do you think politicians should 'look good' on TV?

c Is your parliament televised?

'A GREAT DAY FOR THE ENTERTAINMENT INDUSTRY'

– that's how Conservative MP Norman Tebbitt described the historic televising of the House of Commons last week.

For the first time television cameras were allowed into the House of Commons last Tuesday at 2.30pm and a large barrier between the British people and their elected representatives was broken down within seconds. The British people could for the first time see their members of Parliament at work – debating the points of the day.

True, there has always been the public gallery where any member of the public can come in to view the day's happenings in the House of Commons.

But the public gallery holds 157 people maximum, and what is that compared with the millions of people who can now watch the goings-on in the Houses of Parliament in their own homes?

It is therefore not without reason that the televising of the House of Commons has been called 'a great day for democracy.' The television cameras have opened up the workings of Parliament to the people who voted their representatives into power.

But how far is this true? The first Conservative MP to come under the television spotlight said that he had just received a letter from image consultants keen to improve his image for the cameras.

According to them, the most important thing about an MP was not what he or

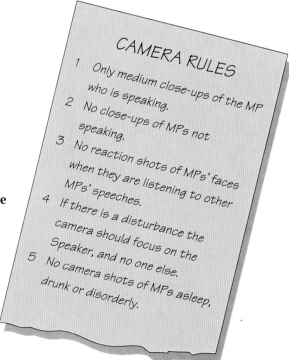

she said, but what they looked like, accounting for a staggering 62 per cent of their overall impact on our screens. There is little doubt that MPs will now be playing to a new audience, not only to each other.

They may try and use the TV medium to win potential viewers' votes, particularly when a general election is in sight. And some people fear that the day may come when we vote MPs in not for what they stand for, but for their presentation and style. Television will become the new hustings – the place where MPs campaign for votes.

Adapted from *Early Times*, 30 November – 6 December 1989

Reading comprehension

2 **a** Is this the first time that the public have seen inside the House of Commons?

b What is the main aim of cameras in Parliament?

c How could MPs use the cameras to their advantage?

d Do you think it is a good idea to have cameras in the Commons?

Interpretation (speaking)

3 **TV cameramen working in the House of Commons have been given a list of rules to follow.**

a Can you think of possible reasons for each rule?

b Do you think the rules are fair, or too strict?

CAMERA RULES

1 Only medium close-ups of the MP who is speaking.

2 No close-ups of MPs not speaking.

3 No reaction shots of MPs' faces when they are listening to other MPs' speeches.

4 If there is a disturbance the camera should focus on the Speaker, and no one else.

5 No camera shots of MPs asleep, drunk or disorderly.

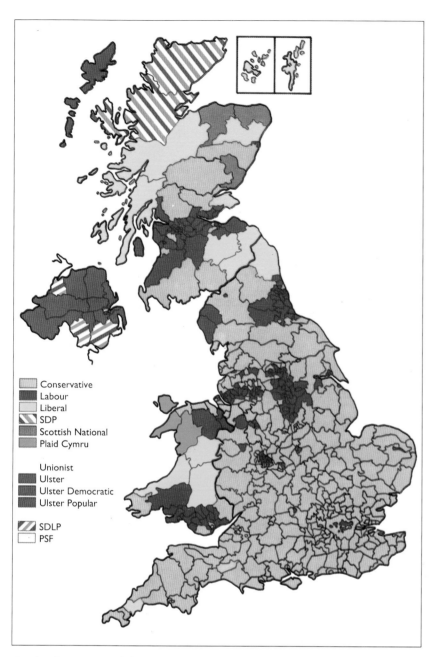

Results of 1987 General Election

Conservative
Labour
Liberal
SDP
Scottish National
Plaid Cymru

Unionist
Ulster
Ulster Democratic
Ulster Popular

SDLP
PSF

ELECTION FEVER

URING a General Election campaign, the media and people in the street talk of little else. Candidates visit their constituencies and speak to people at home, in the streets and at public meetings. Candidates from the major parties often take famous people with them to help persuade voters. Rock groups hold special concerts for the party they support.

The most important MPs and party leaders are on TV day and night. Some pay public relations experts to help them project the right image for the TV cameras – the best clothes, the most convincing smile or the best way to present their policies to the voters. Some critics complain that elections are a 'media circus'. Even the counting of the secret votes is televised 'live' and it can take all night to find out which party has won the most seats, and thus who will be the party in power.

Reading comprehension

4 **a** Describe two things that a candidate could do to win votes.

b Give two reasons for thinking that a British election is a 'media circus'.

c Describe how an election is organised in your country.

Vocabulary

5 **Match each of these words to the correct definition.**

- *general election*
- *candidate*
- *policies*
- *constituency*

Area represented by an MP
The plans of a political party
When the whole country votes for its MPs
Person who is standing for Parliament

Interpretation

6 **a** Which party won the most seats in Parliament in the 1987 election?

b Do you notice any difference in voting patterns in different areas?

In the United Kingdom, general elections are held every few years, when voting takes place in all of the 651 areas or constituencies into which the country is divided. A Member of Parliament is elected to represent each area, and the leader of the party with most Members forms the Government. Between general elections there may be several by-elections.

Voters learn about candidates through the local newspapers and through leaflets which give their background, their views and the policies of their party.

Forming a Government

Pre-reading

1 Read and find out:

    a Who is the Prime Minister?

    b What is the Cabinet?

    c Where does the government meet?

A

C

B

THE CABINET

The party which wins the most seats in the General Election forms the government. The leader of the winning party becomes Prime Minister.

As leaders of their political parties and leaders of the country, Prime Ministers are powerful and important people. They are powerful because they have the majority support in Parliament and they can choose their own ministers and government.

The PM chooses a committee of ministers called the Cabinet. This is made up of a selection of senior MPs from the House of Commons and some members of the House of Lords.

Each member of the Cabinet is a minister responsible for a government department: for example, the Secretary of State for Education and Science is responsible for all the schools, universities and teachers in Britain. The Cabinet of ministers runs the country.

The Cabinet meets at the Prime Minister's house – 10 Downing Street.

The Cabinet works as a team and all ministers must accept the decisions of the 'group'. The team of ministers must always agree in public because they are collectively responsible for the decisions they make. If a minister cannot agree with all the others, he usually resigns from the cabinet. Cabinet meetings are held in private and the details must remain secret for at least 30 years. It has been argued that Margaret Thatcher tried to change this style of cabinet and she was forced to resign when the other ministers could not agree with her.

Cabinet ministers cannot, however, do as they please! They are responsible to Parliament and must answer questions from backbenchers in the House of Commons. Even the Prime Minister must answer questions every Tuesday and Thursday in the Commons – this is called Prime Minister's Question Time and can be one of the most interesting discussions in British politics. Everyone wants to know what has been decided behind the closed doors of the Cabinet Room!

Reading comprehension

2 Read the text and answer TRUE or FALSE.

    a The Prime Minister is the oldest MP.

    b The Prime Minister's party has the most MPs.

    c The Cabinet is chosen by the voters.

    d All Cabinet ministers must agree in public.

    e The Prime Minister does not have to explain his or her actions.

Say what you think might be happening in each of the photographs.

Interpretation

3 Look at the chart opposite and answer the questions.

  a Who does these jobs in your country?

  b Which British minister would do the following jobs?
  – represent Britain at an international meeting;
  – decide how much tax people should pay on their income;
  – announce reforms in the legal system.

  c Which minister works in the following places?
  – at the Foreign Office;
  – next door to the Prime Minister;
  – at the Home Office.

Interpretation

4 a What is the longest period between general elections?

  b Which Prime Minister has spent most time in office?

  c Which two political parties have dominated British politics since 1945?

  d Do you know the name of the present Prime Minister? When was he/she elected?

  e Which political party is in power at the moment?

Activity

5 Use the information on this page to complete the puzzle.

THE MOST IMPORTANT MINISTERS

MINISTER	RESPONSIBILITY
Chancellor of the Exchequer	Government spending Presents the Budget annually in March Lives at 11 Downing Street
Foreign Secretary	Relations with other countries
Home Secretary	Internal relations The police, Law and order (prisons, criminals), law courts

PRIME MINISTERS SINCE 1945

Election	Period of office	Prime Minister	Party
1945	1945-1950	Attlee	Labour
1950	1950-1951	Attlee	Labour
1951	1951-1955	Churchill	Conservative
1955	1955-1957	Eden	Conservative
	1957-1959	Macmillan	Conservative
1959	1959-1963	Macmillan	Conservative
	1963-1964	Home	Conservative
1964	1964-1966	Wilson	Labour
1966	1966-1970	Wilson	Labour
1970	1970-1974	Heath	Conservative
1974	1974-1976	Wilson	Labour
	1976-1979	Callaghan	Labour
1979	1979-1983	Thatcher	Conservative
1983	1983-1987	Thatcher	Conservative
1987	1987-1990	Thatcher	Conservative
	1990-1992	Major	Conservative
1992	1992-	Major	Conservative

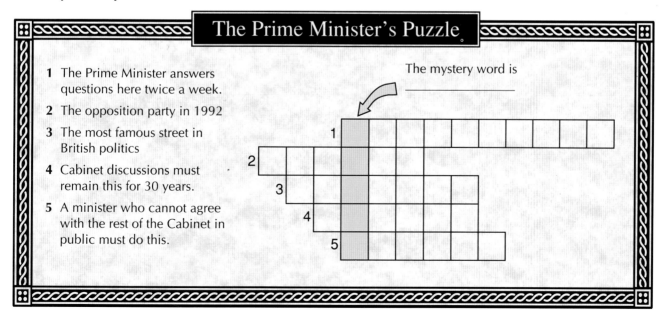

The Prime Minister's Puzzle

1 The Prime Minister answers questions here twice a week.

2 The opposition party in 1992

3 The most famous street in British politics

4 Cabinet discussions must remain this for 30 years.

5 A minister who cannot agree with the rest of the Cabinet in public must do this.

The mystery word is
_____

The potential voters

Reading

1 The teenage magazine *Rage* asked young people in Britain about their voting habits. Three main questions were asked:

a Are you interested in politics?

b Who would you vote for in the next election?

c What would influence the way you vote?

Some of their replies appear opposite.

Discussion

2 **What would make you vote for a politician?**

Appearance	– It's important that the person is well dressed.	☐
Family	– I would vote for a politician my parents support.	☐
Views	– It's important that the person represents the causes I believe in.	☐
Face	– It's important that the politician looks honest.	☐
Friends	– I would vote for a person my friends support.	☐

Tick (✔) the statements that you agree with – you can add others if you wish. Put the statements in order of importance for you.

FACT FILE ACTIVITIES

1 **Politics and parties**

a Write the names of political parties in your country on the chart. Have you got any parties similar to British ones? Are there more parties in your country?

b Write a list of the main policies of *one* party in your country.

2 **Constituencies and parties**

a How many MPs represent the city of Cardiff?

b Do all the MPs for Cardiff have to belong to the same party?

3 **How much do you know about British politics now?**

Complete the two diagrams with the words in the box.

4 **Project work**

Collect as much information as you can about Britain's politicians from your newspapers over a period of time (a month or more). Do they visit your country? What are their names? What impression do they give? Keep a check on your own politicians – have any of them been to Britain recently? Why?

"I don't think about politics. There's no point in worrying about it. It doesn't affect me. I'll decide who to vote for when the time comes. I'm sure it will be Tory."
Charlotte Bale, 15, school student.

"I think politics are important. They determine the kind of society we live in. I think John Major has made a difference. The Tories are more likely to win the next election now. I'd much rather have a Labour government."
Annie Gurney, 14, school student.

"I had politics forced on me. I can remember going on CND marches when I was four, because my parents were a bit right-on. It didn't put me off. I wouldn't go into politics because I'm too shy. But I'd vote for Labour."
Fiona Luck, 15, school student.

"A lot of my college friends were really into green politics and I learnt a lot from them. The greens relate well to young people. John Major has made no difference. He's just a puppet."
Charles Fernandez, 18, window dresser.

"Politics are boring. I'm more interested in fashion and boys. My family vote Tory and I just follow them."
Antonia Runnicles, 15, school student.

"I keep abreast of the news because you have to understand what's going on in the world to be able to change it. I think people are starting to take green politics seriously but it will be a while before they become a viable alternative."
Glen Wilson, 19, between jobs.

Source: *Rage*, Issue 8, 1991

FACT FILE

1

	LEFT		CENTRE		RIGHT	
	Communist Party	Labour Party	Liberal Democrats	Conservative Party	National Front	
Britain						
Your country						

2 Cardiff's elected representatives

Here is a map of Cardiff. The city is divided into four constituencies. Each constituency is represented by one MP.

Cardiff North is represented by Mr Gwilym Jones (Conservative).

Cardiff Central is represented by Ian Grist (Conservative).

Cardiff South and Penarth is represented by Mr Alun Michael (Labour).

Cardiff West is represented by Mr Rhodri Morgan (Labour).

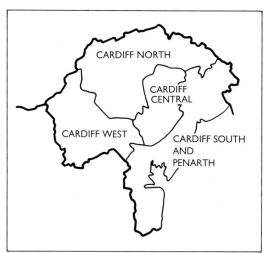

Source: The Parliamentary Education Unit

3

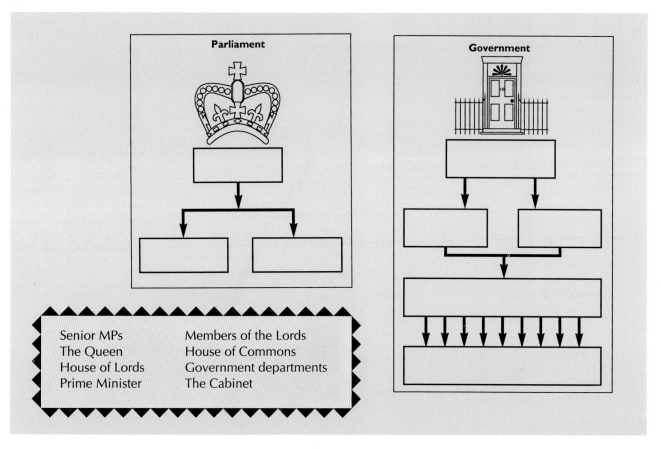

Senior MPs
The Queen
House of Lords
Prime Minister

Members of the Lords
House of Commons
Government departments
The Cabinet

Unit 3

What Britain looks like

Physical features

Pre-reading

1 Complete these texts, using the maps below.

The British Isles

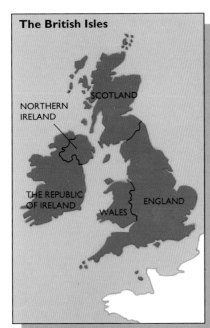

The United Kingdom (or the UK) is a short way of saying the United Kingdom of Great Britain and Northern Ireland. The UK is the political name for those countries which share a parliament in London. All of them were at one time independent kingdoms with their own monarch. Now they are all part of the same kingdom and share the same monarch. The UK consists of ...., ..., ... and ....
.........................The peoples of these countries are British subjects; they hold British passports and therefore their nationality is British. ▼

Great Britain

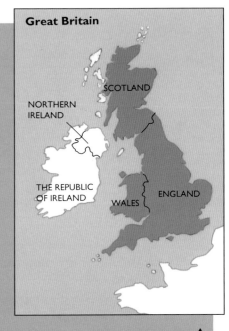

▲

The British Isles is the geographical name for all the islands off the .... coast of Europe. These islands also include the Republic of .... (Eire), which is politically independent of the British government. Many people refer to the inhabitants of the British Isles as 'the English', but England is only one of the countries. The other countries are ...., and ....

The United Kingdom

Great Britain is the name of the one island which is made up of ...., ... and .... It is called Great because in some languages the word for Britain (Bretagne) is the same as the word for Brittany, which is in France. The word 'Great' helps to distinguish the two: 'Grande Bretagne' = Great Britain, 'Bretagne' = Brittany.

Reading comprehension

2 Answer YES or NO.

a Do the people of Eire hold British passports?

b Is Scotland part of the UK?

c Is Northern Ireland part of Great Britain?

Find the information

3 Complete this table, using the map opposite.

Country	Capital	Mountains	Rivers
England			
Scotland			
Wales			
N. Ireland			

Reading

COUNTIES AND CONURBATIONS

Britain is divided into 53 areas called **counties**. (You can see these areas on the map on the front cover of this book.) The counties around the capital, London, are known as the Home Counties. Some large cities have become highly populated and have expanded into the surrounding countryside. These large urban areas are known as **conurbations**. Greater Manchester is a conurbation that includes the industrial city of Manchester, all its suburbs and the surrounding towns which form a single urban mass.

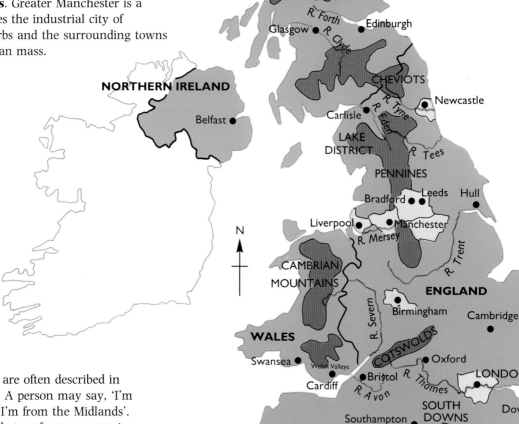

Different parts of Britain are often described in terms of compass points. A person may say, 'I'm from the North-east' or 'I'm from the Midlands'. Alternatively, it is possible to refer to an area in terms of its geographical features, for example, 'The Lake District' or 'The Welsh Valleys'.

Reading comprehension

4 a Divide these words into *country* or *county*.

Kent   Scotland   Wales   Essex   England
Cornwall

b Which of these counties are Home Counties?

Kent   Surrey   Norfolk   Berkshire
Yorkshire   Essex

c Match each of these towns with its correct area.

AREA	TOWN/CITY
The Midlands	Brighton
The North-east	Inverness
The Highlands	Birmingham
The South-east	Newcastle

d Read the clues and identify the city.

This Scottish city is on the river Clyde.
This large port is in south-west England, on the river Avon.
This is the capital city of Wales.

e Now write two more clues to test your classmates.

Energy sources

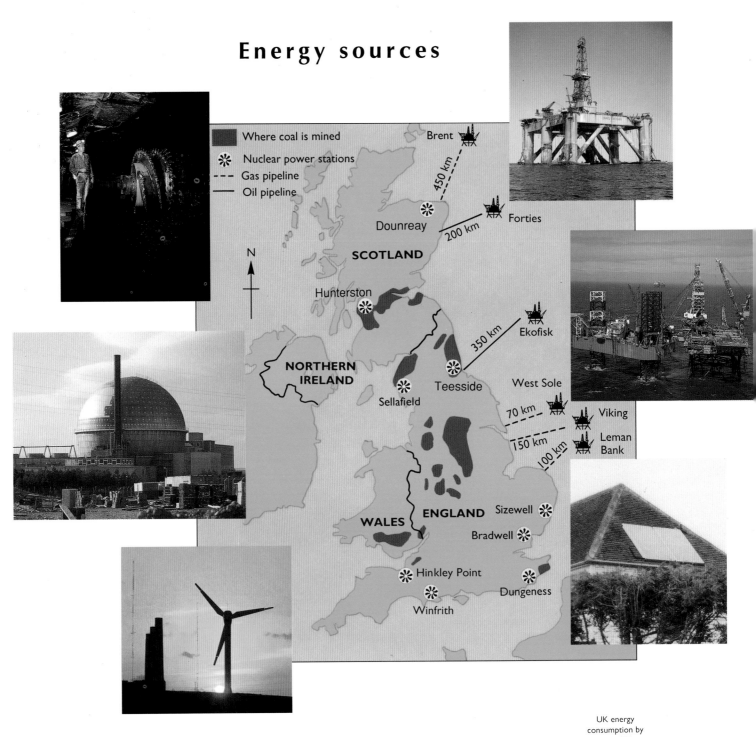

Where coal is mined
* Nuclear power stations
--- Gas pipeline
— Oil pipeline

Brent
450 km
Dounreay
200 km
Forties
SCOTLAND
N
Hunterston
Ekofisk
350 km
NORTHERN IRELAND
Teesside
West Sole
Sellafield
70 km
Viking
150 km
Leman Bank
100 km
ENGLAND
Sizewell
WALES
Bradwell
Hinkley Point
Dungeness
Winfrith

UK energy consumption by fuel, 1990

Coke, breeze & other solid fuels
Coke oven gas
Coal
Petroleum
Natural gas
Electricity

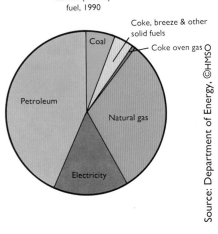

Pre-reading

1 Before you read, look at the photos above and answer the questions.

  a Which form of energy is the cleanest?

  b Which form of energy is the cheapest?

  c Which of these energy sources do you use in your home?

  d What are the main energy sources in your country?

2 Now study the map and complete these sentences.

  a Coal is mined in the Midlands, _____

  b Oil can be found under _____

  c Nuclear power stations are generally located on

  _____

20

Source: Department of Energy, ©HMSO

THE ENERGY DEBATE

nuclear power

Britain in the 1990s is concerned about producing too little or too much energy. It relies heavily on four main types of energy: oil, coal, gas and **nuclear power**.

coal industry
mined
Industrial
  Revolution
heavy industries
shipbuilding
next century
pollution

Coal and industry Britain's **coal industry** is one of the largest and most technologically advanced in Western Europe. Coal has been **mined** in Britain since Roman times but became particularly important during the eighteenth and nineteenth centuries; the **Industrial Revolution** was powered by coal, and large cities and **heavy industries** (such as steel and **shipbuilding**) developed in the areas where coal was found, which are still among the most heavily populated areas in Britain today. Coal is certainly Britain's cheapest energy source, and supplies should last into the **next century**. However, excessive coal burning has contributed to acid rain and **pollution** in Britain, as it is the dirtiest form of energy.

transport
distribution
discovery
self-sufficient
economy
refineries
drilling rigs
pipelines
endangers
safety

Economic self-sufficiency Oil has become increasingly vital to Britain's **transport** and **distribution** systems and, until the 1970s, most of it was imported from the Middle East. However, the **discovery** of oil, along with natural gas, in the North Sea in 1970 has enabled Britain to become **self-sufficient** in these energy sources. The high-quality oil has boosted Britain's **economy** and created jobs, particularly on the north-east coast of Scotland near the oil rigs and **refineries**. Britain has, however, had to invest heavily in the construction of **drilling rigs** and the maintenance of deep sea **pipelines**, and conservationists protest that oil pollutes the coastal waters and **endangers** fishing in the North Sea.

Is nuclear power safe? Many Britons are also concerned about the **safety** of Britain's nuclear power stations. Britain has had a nuclear energy programme since 1955, and nearly all the money spent on energy research has been concentrated on nuclear power. There are now sixteen nuclear power stations, located in relatively unpopulated coastal areas and away from large cities. Nevertheless, there has been one serious accident at Sellafield nuclear power station in Cumbria in 1957, and the incidence of **leukaemia** - a cancer of the blood - around several British nuclear power stations is much higher than normal, particularly in children.

leukaemia

debate
different supplies

dangers
environment
aware

Where next? The **debate** continues in the 1990s. Which energy source is the safest and cleanest? Which is the cheapest? The government wishes to maintain all the **different supplies** of energy as it is dangerous to rely too much on one single source. The arguments against using certain fuels such as coal, or using nuclear power, all emphasise the **dangers** of these energy sources to Britain's **environment**. Since the 1980s Britons have become much more environmentally **aware**, and it looks as if the energy debate will continue well into the next century.

Reading comprehension

3 a Use the text to make notes.

Energy source	Advantages	Disadvantages
coal		*dirty*
oil		
nuclear power		

b Tick (✔) a,b or c.

i Britain's oldest source of energy is ......
  a North Sea oil.
  b gas.
  c coal.

ii Britain's most recent discovery is ....
  a coal in South Wales.
  b oil in the North Sea.
  c nuclear power.

iii The energy debate is about...................
  a which energy source to use.
  b North Sea oil.
  c safety in nuclear power plants.

Writing

4 a Draw a map of your country and mark the energy sources on the map.

  b Find out about your country's main sources – does it use mainly oil? Does it buy oil or coal? Are there any nuclear power stations? Does your country depend on one type of energy?

  c Write a paragraph to describe energy sources in your country.

  d Are people in your country concerned about pollution and the environment?

The British climate

Pre-reading

1 **Here are some common ideas that people have about the weather in Britain. Tick (✔) those you have heard. Are they true?**

It rains all the time – it is very damp.

There's terrible fog in London, just like in Sherlock Holmes.

The sun never shines in July or August.

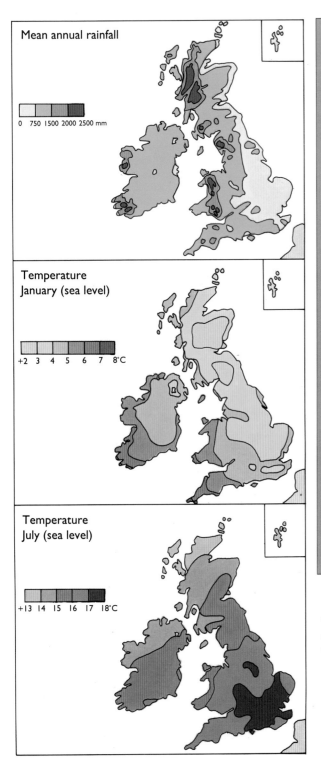

Mean annual rainfall

0 750 1500 2000 2500 mm

Temperature January (sea level)

+2 3 4 5 6 7 8°C

Temperature July (sea level)

+13 14 15 16 17 18°C

THE BRITISH CLIMATE

Britain has a variable climate. The weather changes so frequently that it is difficult to forecast. It is not unusual for people to complain that the weathermen were wrong. Fortunately, as Britain does not experience extreme weather conditions, it is never very cold or very hot. The temperature rarely rises above 32°C (90°F) in summer, or falls below –10°C (14°F) in winter.

Summers are generally cool, but due to global warming they are starting to get drier and hotter. Newspapers during a hot spell talk of 'heatwaves' and an 'Indian summer' (dry, hot weather in September or October). Hot weather causes terrible congestion on the roads as Britons rush to the coastal resorts.

Winters are generally mild, with the most frequent and prolonged snowfalls in the Scottish Highlands, where it is possible to go skiing. If it does snow heavily in other parts of Britain, the country often comes to a standstill. Trains, buses and planes are late. People enjoy discussing the snow, complaining about the cold and comparing the weather conditions with previous winters!

Contrary to popular opinion, it does not rain all the time. There is certainly steady rainfall throughout most of the year, but the months from September to January are the wettest. Thanks to the rain, Britain has a richly fertile countryside which is famous for its deep green colour.

Since the 1950s, most British cities have introduced clean air zones. Factories and houses cannot burn coal and must use smokeless fuel. The dirt caused by smoke used to cause terrible fogs, particularly in London. Londoners used to call their fogs 'London Particulars' or 'pea-soupers' (as thick as pea soup) and you could not see your hand in front of you. Such fogs are now a thing of the past, but you can still see them in old films where they add mystery and atmosphere to murder stories and thrillers!

Reading comprehension

2 a **Answer TRUE or FALSE.**

   i The weather in Britain is the same most of the time.

   ii Winters are not excessively cold.

   iii Britain frequently has 'Indian summers'.

   iv Pea-soupers are a serious problem in London.

b **Use the weather maps to answer these questions.**

   i Which is warmer in summer, northern or southern England?

   ii Which part of Britain has the coldest winters?

   iii Which coast would you choose for a day at the beach in July?

Talking about the weather

People often say that the British talk about the weather all the time. This is an exaggeration, but it is certainly true that the weather is a good way to start a conversation with a stranger. If your climate was as variable as Britain's, you would certainly talk about the strange changes too! The weather is a neutral topic of conversation which is very useful when visiting Britain.

A

B

3 Match these common conversational openers with the appropriate weather type.

Expression

Weather conditions

I like a bit of sun, don't you?

Nice day, isn't it?

What a miserable day, isn't it?

I'm boiling!

Brr, it's freezing, isn't it?

What a scorcher!

It must be minus 2 today!

What terrible showers we're having!

It hasn't snowed like this since 1963!

I'm soaked through!

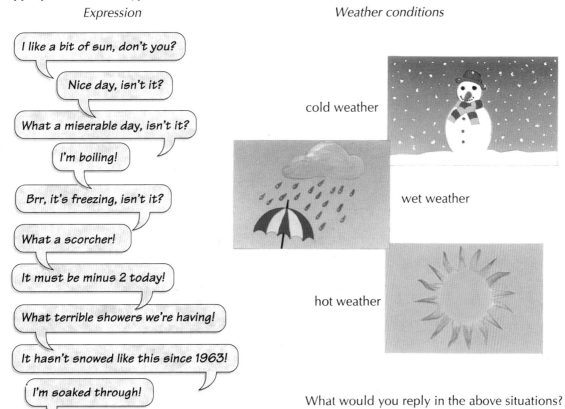

cold weather

wet weather

hot weather

What would you reply in the above situations?

23

ROUND BRITAIN QUIZ

1 Which sea separates England from Ireland?
   a the North Sea b the Atlantic Ocean c the Irish Sea

2 Where are Britain's oil rigs?
   a the Channel b the North Sea c the Atlantic

3 How many countries make up Great Britain?
   a four b three c five

4 What nationality are the people of Northern Ireland?
   a English b Irish c British

5 In which country is the Lake District?
   a Scotland b England c Wales

6 Where are Britain's ski resorts?
   a the Pennines b the Cheviots c the Scottish Highlands

7 What is the climate in Britain like?
   a tropical b changeable c Arctic

8 Where are most of Britain's coal mines?
   a on the coasts b in the South-east c inland

9 Which of these countries has road signs in two languages?
   a England b Scotland c Wales

10 Rainfall in Britain is heaviest in
   a autumn and winter b winter and spring
   c spring and summer

FACT FILE

BIGGEST CITY : London

LONGEST RIVER :
   The Severn (354 km)

HIGHEST PEAK : Ben Nevis,
   Scotland (1,343 m)

LARGEST LAKE : Lough Neagh,
   N. Ireland (388 sq km)

WETTEST AREAS : The North
   and West

WARMEST AREA : The South-east

	England		Scotland		Wales		N. Ireland
Capital		London		Edinburgh		Cardiff	Belfast
Population		47,689,000		5,091,000		2,873,000	1,583,000
Language	English (also used as official language in more than sixty other countries).		English is spoken throughout Scotland. Scots Gaelic (an ancient Celtic language) is still spoken today by 80,000 people, names have a long history and the Scots belong to clans (ancient family groups) each of which has its own tartan (distinctively patterned cloth).		19% of the population speak Welsh, which is a language of Celtic origin. Since the 1960s, efforts to promote the use of the Welsh language have increased. Road signs are in both English and Welsh and, on television, Channel 4 Wales shows programmes in Welsh. It is the medium of instruction in Welsh schools, and is also studied at university.		English is the main language but Irish Gaelic (a Celtic language) is spoken. Over 20,000 secondary school pupils study Gaelic, and the two universities in Northern Ireland offer degree courses and research in Gaelic.

Tourist areas

England	Scotland	Wales	N. Ireland
London is popular with overseas visitors. The most visited attractions are: Madame Tussauds, the Tower of London and the British Museum. Areas associated with English writers: Warwickshire (Shakespeare), the Lake District (William Wordsworth – poet), Yorkshire (the Brontë sisters – novelists) and Dorset (Thomas Hardy – novelist). Devon and Cornwall (the West Country) are also very popular. Natural attractions: 34 Areas of Outstanding Natural Beauty, 6 Forest Parks and 7 National Parks	The annual Edinburgh Festival is one of the world's leading cultural events. Glasgow was European City of Culture in 1990. Golf originated in Scotland and golfing and outdoor holidays are popular. Salmon fishing is excellent and many visitors come to see the world famous whisky distilleries. Skiing in the Highlands at Aviemore is popular. The scenic beauty of Scotland's hills, mountains and castles is renowned.	Wales is particularly popular for outdoor holidays and the national music and literature festival, Eisteddfod, is a major attraction. There are 3 National Parks – Snowdonia, the Brecon Beacons and the Pembrokeshire Coast.	Despite its reputation for political troubles, Northern Ireland is very beautiful and attracts more and more tourists every year. Americans show great interest (many, including some former Presidents of the USA, are of Irish descent). The annual Belfast Festival is the second largest international festival in Britain. The Glens (valleys) of Antrim and the Giant's Causeway are two main tourist areas. The Causeway, on the Antrim coast, consists of 40,000 stone columns leading from the cliffs to the sea. Irish whiskey is popular.

Living in Britain

Cities

A magazine in Britain recently asked its readers to give their opinion of Britain's ten biggest cities: Glasgow, Edinburgh, Liverpool, London, Leeds, Birmingham, Sheffield, Manchester, Bristol and Bradford. Here are some of their replies.

ENVIRONMENT

THINGS TO DO

CULTURE

STREET SAFETY

CLEANLINESS

PUBLIC TRANSPORT

FRIENDLINESS

LOCAL MEN

NIGHTLIFE

JOB OPPORTUNITIES

PROPERTY

SHOPPING

OPEN SPACES

EDINBURGH
according to Xenia Koning, 27

'There's clean, fresh air, plus the facilities of a capital city.'

'Many bars open late, so it's a very relaxed way of life.'

'My only complaint is there's not enough time to see it all!'

'The main problem is drunken men – when men here drink they radiate aggression.'

'Edinburgh is always very clean and litter-free.'

'I have no complaints as far as transport is concerned.'

'People are friendly but a bit reserved.'

'Although they look good, the men are macho.'

'To be honest, nightlife in the city is a bit lacking.'

'It's not bad in the city centre, but unemployment's rife elsewhere.'

'House prices are among the highest in Scotland.'

'Excellent, though there are few markets and stalls.'

'There are many hills, parks and green areas.'

LIVERPOOL
according to Joanne Lloyd, 18

'It's pretty poor, with litter and endless roadworks.'

'There's a sports centre in every town.'

'It's a cosmopolitan city, especially around Albert Dock.'

'You wouldn't walk alone at night. You're always reading about attacks.'

'Pretty poor – the streets are always grubby and littered.'

'Liverpool is well served by rail, though it's expensive.'

'People are *very* friendly – even complete strangers.'

'I avoid the young ones; men are better in their twenties!'

'It's a problem – clubs get crowded at weekends.'

'It depends on what kind of job you want – it's not great for top jobs.'

'You can get a terraced house for just £15,000.'

'Good – there are lots of new precincts.'

'Sefton Park is the lungs of Liverpool.'

Source: *Company*, November 1990

Reading activity

1 a Answer TRUE or FALSE.

  i   The environment is better in Edinburgh than in Liverpool.
  ii Liverpool is cleaner than Edinburgh.
  iii People are friendlier in Liverpool than in Edinburgh.
  iv Homes are cheaper in Liverpool than in Edinburgh.

b Write the questions that you think the interviewer asked.

c Here are some replies for Bristol. Match each of them to the correct category of question.

  i   'It's very expensive – about £50,000 for a small flat.'
  ii 'There are bins everywhere and the shops are kept nicely.'
  iii 'I don't feel safe on my own or even in a group after 9 pm.'
  iv 'The last bus to where I live is at 10 pm!'

Vocabulary

2 a Match the adjectives on the left with their opposites on the right.

b Now try to write the comparative form of each adjective.

c Write two sentences comparing Bristol with Liverpool or Edinburgh.

friendly	dirty
clean	expensive
crowded	badly situated
beautiful	dark
cheap	reserved
littered	deserted
well-lit	ugly
exciting	litter-free
well situated	boring

Writing and speaking

3 a Write a sentence about your town/city or village under each of the categories in the table.

	YOUR TOWN
ENVIRONMENT	
THINGS TO DO	
SHOPPING	
PUBLIC TRANSPORT	

b Interview your partner about his/her town.

Housing

Pre-reading

1 **Look at the pictures of British homes below and answer:**

   a Which type of house do you think is the cheapest? Which is the most expensive?

   b Where do you think you would see each type of house?
      city centre   suburb   outskirts of a town/city   in the countryside   by the sea

   c What sort of person do you think would live in each type of house?
      poor   average   well-off(affluent)   rich   super-rich

Reading activity

2 Read these descriptions of British homes. As you read the text, match each type of house with the correct picture. Which photograph is *not* mentioned in the text? Why do you think this is?

KEY WORDS	
terraced houses	**Terraced houses** are usually found in inner cities. They can be anything up to 150 years old and were often built by industries to house their workers near the factories. They are built in long rows where each house is attached to the ones on either side. The back of this type of house faces the back of another identical row of houses, so they are often known as 'back to backs'. In recent years many terraced houses have been renovated; central heating has been added and other improvements made to what was originally a simple and sometimes primitive home with an outside toilet and no bathroom.
semi-detached houses	**Semi-detached houses** have been built in large numbers since the 1930s, when Britain's towns and cities expanded into suburbs. Each house is part of a pair and is joined on one side to its partner. The semi usually has a small back and front garden, three bedrooms and a small bathroom. It is the most popular type of house in Britain and could be called the home of **'Mr and Mrs Average'**. Towns in Britain have areas which contain streets and streets of semis, often with well-kept gardens.
Mr and Mrs Average	
detached house	The **detached house** stands by itself, usually with a garden all around it. These houses are much more expensive than semis and are often owned by professional people. Most detached houses are to be found in affluent suburbs or in the 'green belt' – a strip of protected open countryside around a city, where no industrial development or major building schemes are allowed. Some large cities (particularly London) also have a 'commuter belt' – so called because the professionals who live there travel (commute) every day to work into the city by train or car. London is surrounded by miles and miles of 'commuter belt'. Some commuters travel up to three or four hours a day to get from their homes to the inner city.

country cottages	Britain is famous for its **country cottages** which were often built on the country estates of wealthy landowners. The workers on the estate rented the cottages from the landowner and worked on the land. Cottages were also frequently built around a village green. Cottages have low ceilings, wooden beams and sometimes a thatched roof. In recent years some cottages have become second homes, bought by professionals during the economic boom of the 1980s.
tower blocks	In the 1950s and 1960s local councils cleared a lot of the slums in the inner city areas and knocked down terraced houses in very poor areas. The people were re-housed in tower blocks on the outskirts of the city or in the centre of the city. **Tower blocks** can vary from 3-5 storeys high up to 10-20 storeys high. Each storey contains 5 or 6 flats for families. In recent years local councils have tried to improve the areas around tower blocks by creating 'green space', children's playgrounds and facilities for the community to use. Some tower blocks in large cities like London can be very dangerous at night and they have been criticised for their long dark corridors, which encourage crime and vandalism.

Reading comprehension

3 a Tick (✔) the correct answer.

   i Terraced houses can be mainly found **a** in the country. ☐
                                             b near industries. ☐
                                             c in the suburbs. ☐

   ii Cottages can mainly be found **a** in green places. ☐
                                             b in country villages. ☐
                                             c in the suburbs. ☐

   iii Tower blocks were built for **a** small families. ☐
                                           b large families ☐
                                           c a large number of families. ☐

b Use the text to label this diagram of a British city.

   i Complete the key to the parts of the city. Use these words:

   suburbs   city centre (inner city)   commuter belt   outskirts

   ii Write down the types of houses you are most likely to see in each part of the city.

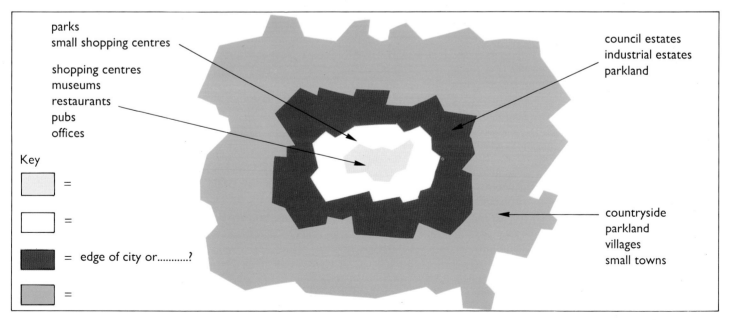

Activity

4 Describe the different types of apartment or house in your country. How do they compare with the average British home?

Taking action

Pre-reading

1 a **Label each picture with the correct word:**

aerosols (containing CFCs)   plastic carrier bags
car exhaust fumes (lead in petrol)
hunting   tree cutting (deforestation)   litter

b **Each one of these objects or activities can be harmful(dangerous) to the environment or surroundings. Why and how?**

1

2

6

5

4

3

Read and find out

2 **According to the text, what**

a are pressure groups?   **b** are 'green issues'?   **c** has happened in Britain in the last ten years?

KEY WORDS	**PUBLIC ATTITUDES**
	People in Britain like to feel they can 'have a say' in how their town is planned and how their
pressure groups	surroundings are protected. Britain has a long tradition of **pressure groups** and **voluntary**
voluntary	**organisations** which work towards finding solutions to problems in the country or their area.
organisations	Pressure groups try to persuade the government, local councils or companies, to change plans or

laws, to 'take action'. In the late 1980s, residents in the South-east organised themselves into a pressure group to stop the government building a railway line from the Channel Tunnel to London because they believed that it would damage the countryside and wildlife in their part of the world. The campaign was successful and the railway was built in a different area.

Voluntary organisations employ people who will work for nothing to help others in their area. One such example is the work of the National Trust which organised a campaign called 'Enterprise Neptune' to protect the coastline in Britain and the rare birds that live there. Thousands of people have worked since 1965 to clean beaches, repair footpaths and raise money so that the National Trust can buy areas of coast that would otherwise be destroyed by roads, buildings and factories. Voluntary organisations also include groups of people who work in the community with the old, the sick and the young. Membership of these organisations has increased by over 50% in the last ten years, particularly in areas relating to **'green' issues** like pollution, saving wildlife and protecting the environment. Prince Charles and other prominent national figures frequently speak in public and on TV and write in the press about the importance of green issues. Even the average person in the street generally believes in doing something to improve the lives of everyone in our society. If there is a problem, it is common to hear people say, 'There should be a law against it', or 'Someone should do something about it!'. This fundamental belief in civic duty is an important part of British culture, even if not all Britons 'take action'.

green issues

CASE STUDY – Tower block residents v British Rail

ROBIN NOWACKI

Room with a view: Lilian Taylor overlooks the viaduct that comes to within four metres of Canterbury House

BR will take you closer

Trevor Barnes talks to residents who'll soon be able to see eye to eye with cross-Channel commuters

The Independent, 4 July 1991

THERE'S close and there's very close. This is very close.

When the Channel tunnel opens in two years' time, up to 1,600 passengers an hour leaving Waterloo International for the Continent will be able to share uninterrupted views of June Beckett's kitchen and bedroom.

She, in turn, will have the pleasure of knowing that from her second-floor balcony she is as near as it is physically possible to be to one of the biggest civil engineering feats of the decade. Twelve feet, in fact.

But for her, and the other residents of Canterbury House, just south of the Thames, delight at the prospect of rubbing shoulders with greatness is offset by the sight and sounds of a viaduct-widening scheme that has cast everything below second-floor level into permanent shade, and replaced one of the few areas of green space in a congested part of the capital with a concrete monolith planted literally on their doorstep.

"They knocked down our pub to make way for it," says Lilian Taylor, who has lived at No 26 with her husband and teenage son for 14 years. "A real old London pub.

And they took away our community centre. We've got nothing now." Nothing, that is, except for the viaduct, four metres away at its nearest point.

The residents here have lived happily with the railways most of their lives. A number come from railway families and have become used to the daily clatter of commuter trains. "I'd miss them if they weren't there," says Dorothy Phillips at No 74, "but to bring them this close is ridiculous. People can't believe their eyes when they come round."

Even normally taciturn businessmen commuting from Guildford and Woking have been seen to lay their newspapers aside and exchange looks of disbelief. British Rail has fitted the flats

with double glazing, but that has had only a marginal impact on the noise. And it has not stopped Lynn Adams's three-year-old son coming into her room in tears every morning saying someone is outside tapping on his bedroom window. There is not, but with workmen just yards from his pillow it seems that way.

"What will it be like when the trains start up?" Mrs Adams wonders — at No 20, the closest of them all. "We don't get any privacy as it is and we have to keep the curtains drawn until we leave for work."

BR acknowledges the railway has come "that little bit closer", but has no plans for compensation. A spokesman says: "Net curtains are not difficult to put up."

The official brochure shows Waterloo International, "London's Gateway to Europe", neatly sited "in its urban context". An aerial photo looks down on Canterbury House, suggesting that the tower block and railway track interlock with majestic harmony. Two floors up, at eye level, it all looks rather different. Europe may be coming closer, but so are the trains.

Reading comprehension

3 Answer the questions.

a Why do the residents of Canterbury House keep their curtains closed during the day?

b Why will passengers on the Channel Tunnel train be able to see June Beckett's kitchen and bedroom?

c Why did British Rail demolish Lilian Taylor's local pub?

d What are British Rail going to do about the problem?

e How do the residents of Canterbury House feel – happy? sad? angry? worried? not bothered?

f What advice would you give the residents of Canterbury House?

Problem solving – letter writing

4 June Beckett has set up a pressure group with the other residents in her tower block and people from nearby houses and blocks. They plan to campaign for compensation and this newspaper article is their first action. Now they are going to write to British Rail.

  a Working in groups, write a letter from the Canterbury House Residents' Association to British Rail. Explain your problems again and ask for some form of compensation. Remember to be polite, clear and write simple sentences.

  b Give your letter to another group of students. Write British Rail's reply.

FACT FILE ACTIVITIES

1 Try to answer the following questions.

  a Who are the Friends of the Earth?

  b Why do you think durable bags are better than plastic bags?

  c What do you think a zebra crossing is?

  d What campaign methods can children use to improve the environment?

2 Look at the posters and literature advertising pressure groups in Britain. What do you think each of the groups campaigns for?

3 Look at the table opposite.

  a Underline any of the facts which are not the same in your country.

  b Does anything surprise you? Why?

  c Do people in your country prefer to live in flats or houses? Do they prefer to rent or buy their homes?

4 Working in small groups, discuss the following questions:

  a Are there any pressure groups or voluntary organisations in your country or area? What types of campaign do they organise?

  b What could you do to improve the environment and the surroundings in your town? Make a plan of action.

FACT FILE

1

Taking action

ALL OVER Britain young people are leading the way in persuading others to improve their surroundings. At Muswell Hill in London, a group of children got together and formed the first Junior Friends of the Earth which now has over 150 members. They are going to campaign to get supermarkets to give away durable bags instead of plastic ones, following a survey of the number of plastic carriers given away. They also plan to petition for a zebra crossing to make a local street safer for children. They campaign for change by setting a good example and then explaining to others what they are doing.

3 Housing in Britain

- Most Britons prefer to live in a house rather than in a flat.
- In 1989 65 per cent of people in Britain owned their own home.
- Britons move house more often than people in other European countries.
- Most Britons do not have a second home.
- The British are very proud of their gardens.
- Most local councils have flats and houses for poorer people to rent.
- In 1990 there were 170 000 homeless households in Britain.
- House prices rose steeply during the mid-1980s.
- Most Britons buy their homes with the help of a mortgage (loan) from a building society or bank.
- The average mortgage lasts for 20-25 years.

Transport

Travelling around Britain

1 **Look at the map and diagram and answer the questions.**

a Where do most visitors to Britain arrive? South-west/North-east North-west/South-east

b How many airports can you find near London?

c Name two cross-Channel ports.

d Name two London stations for travellers to the North.

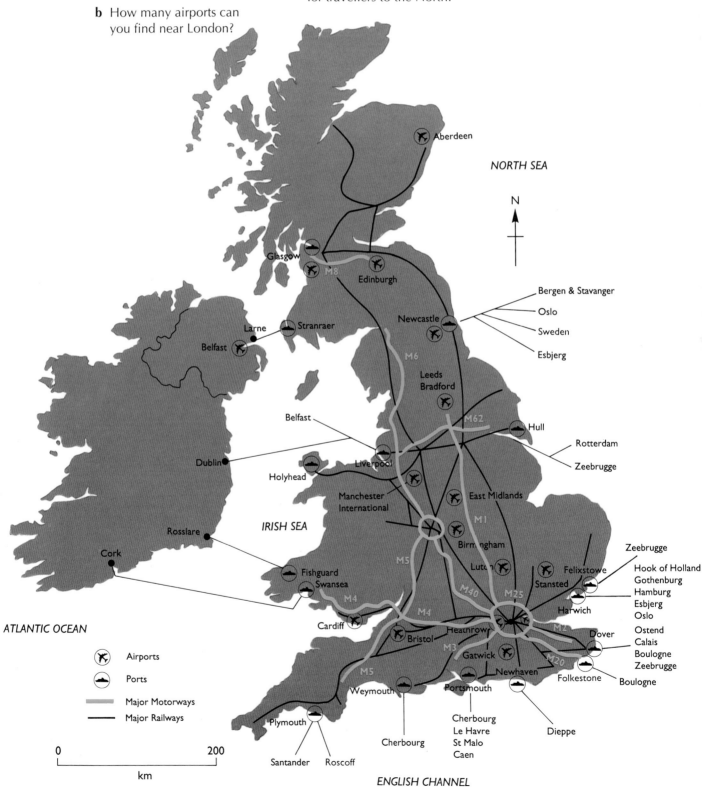

NORTH SEA

N

Aberdeen

Bergen & Stavanger
Oslo
Sweden
Esbjerg

Glasgow
M8
Edinburgh

Newcastle

Larne
Stranraer
Belfast

M6

Leeds
Bradford

Belfast

M62
Hull
Rotterdam
Zeebrugge

Dublin
Liverpool
Holyhead

Manchester
International

East Midlands
M1

IRISH SEA

Rosslare

Cork

Birmingham
Luton

M5

Fishguard
Swansea

M4

Cardiff

M40

M25

Zeebrugge
Felixstowe
Stansted

Hook of Holland
Gothenburg
Hamburg
Esbjerg
Oslo

Harwich

ATLANTIC OCEAN

M4

Heathrow
Bristol
M3
Gatwick

M23

M20

Dover

Ostend
Calais
Boulogne
Zeebrugge

Folkestone
Boulogne

Newhaven

M5

Weymouth
Portsmouth

Dieppe

Plymouth

Cherbourg

Cherbourg
Le Havre
St Malo
Caen

Santander   Roscoff

ENGLISH CHANNEL

✈ Airports

⚓ Ports

▬▬ Major Motorways

─── Major Railways

0 ─────────── 200
km

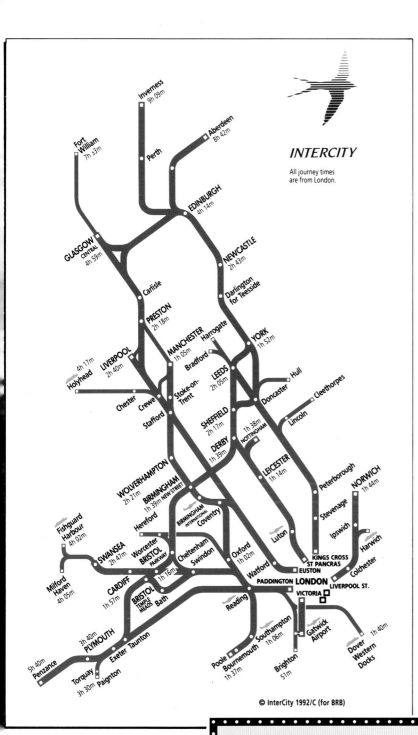

INTERCITY

All journey times are from London.

© InterCity 1992/C (for BRB)

3   Transport in Britain

the oldest motorway

the M1

the busiest airport

London Heathrow

the oldest railway

the Stockton and Darlington

the most recent London airport

London City Airport

the fastest train

the Intercity 125

the fastest plane

Concorde

the most popular form of transport

the car

Interpretation

2   How fast can you complete this quiz? Use the map and diagram to help you.

ROUND BRITAIN QUIZ

a If you wanted to visit Northern Ireland by car, which English or Scottish ferry port would you choose?

b If you fly by charter to Gatwick and take the train to central London, which main-line railway station do you go to if you need to catch a train to Sheffield?

c How long would these journeys take by train? (Allow 40 minutes for crossing London by underground in the rush hour.)
   Southampton – Aberdeen   hours.
   Dover – Edinburgh   hours.

d Describe four ways to get from London to Paris – write the names of the stations/airports/ports ...

Now write a question to test the rest of your class!

TRANSPORT REVOLUTION – PROBLEMS AND SOLUTIONS

This diagram shows some of the problems facing British cities in the 1980s and early 1990s.

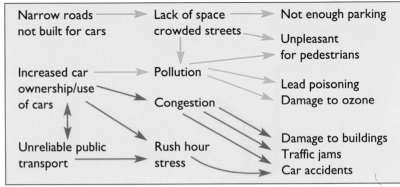

Narrow roads not built for cars → Lack of space crowded streets → Not enough parking

Lack of space crowded streets → Unpleasant for pedestrians

Increased car ownership/use of cars → Pollution → Unpleasant for pedestrians

Pollution → Lead poisoning / Damage to ozone

Increased car ownership/use of cars → Congestion

Unreliable public transport ↔ Increased car ownership/use of cars

Unreliable public transport → Rush hour stress

Congestion → Damage to buildings / Traffic jams / Car accidents

Rush hour stress → Damage to buildings / Traffic jams / Car accidents

Pre-reading

1 a Use the notes in the diagram to write sentences:

Examples: *Too much traffic in city centres causes congestion.*

Too many people driving to work creates rush-hour jams and parking problems.

b Tick (✔) those problems which are shared by cities in your country. Can you think of any possible solutions? Working in pairs, make a list, e.g. *Ban the use of cars in city centres.*

Reading activity

2 Read these descriptions of new transport schemes in Britain. Each scheme aims to offer a solution to one of the problems above.

a Explain which problem(s) each scheme addresses.

b How successful have they been?

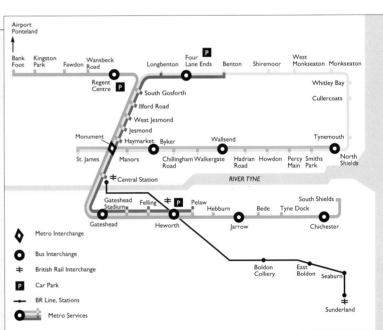

SCHEME A

The Newcastle Metro opened in 1980 and it was Britain's first **fully integrated transport system.** This type of system links buses with 'super trams' to form a complete network. Suburbs, commuter areas and city centres are covered by metro trains which travel underground in the city centre and overground outside. One ticket can be used on both buses and metro trains, and each suburban metro station has free parking facilities. Commuters drive to a station outside the centre and leave their cars, completing their journey into the centre by metro.

A study in 1982 revealed that traffic density in the centre of Newcastle was much lighter than in outer areas. There were more pedestrians, and shops in the centre reported more customers and better sales. Manchester, Birmingham, Bristol, Cardiff and other British cities are now looking at similar schemes.

SCHEME B

In the past, motorists wishing to travel, e.g. from Kent or Hampshire to the Midlands or the North of England, had to drive through London, which greatly increased the existing traffic congestion in the capital. The journey between Heathrow and Gatwick airports was also slow and difficult because there was no direct road link between the two.

In order to relieve these problems the M25 London Orbital Motorway was constructed and completed in 1986. At 120 miles (192km) in circumference it is the world's biggest ring road, and is linked directly with all other motorways and major roads to all parts of Britain. Unfortunately the planners of the M25 seriously underestimated the volume of traffic which would use the new road; they had expected about 80 000 vehicles a day, whereas actual use is nearer 160 000 vehicles a day with all the attendant problems of congestion, pollution, serious accidents and damage to the road surface. One record traffic jam was 35km long in all three lanes. The government is now considering a scheme to build another 'outer' motorway to relieve congestion on the M25!

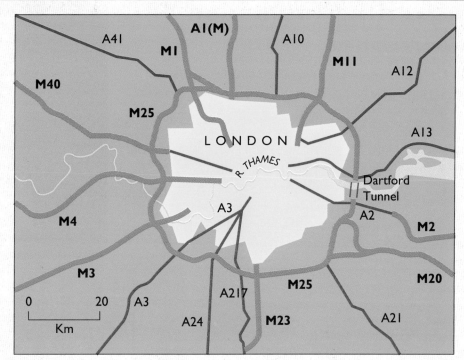

Discussion

3 **What effects do you think the following schemes would have on city transport problems?**

Switching from leaded to unleaded petrol
(Sales of unleaded petrol increased from 0% to 40% in Britain between 1987 and 1990.)

Pedestrian precincts
Many British cities, e.g. York, have banned cars from central areas.

_____

_____

_____

_____

_____

_____

_____

_____

_____

Reading and speaking

4 **How car-dependent are you?**

Complete this questionnaire for yourself. Then compare your answers with a partner's and with the rest of the class. Draw a graph to show the results, e.g. what percentage of your class comes to school by car etc.

> TRANSPORT SURVEY
>
> 1) How do you travel to school?
>   Car ☐ Bus ☐ Train ☐ Bike ☐ Walk ☐
>
> 2) How do you travel to see friends?
>   Car ☐ Bus ☐ Train ☐ Bike ☐ Walk ☐
>
> 3) Which way do you prefer to travel and why?
>   Car ☐ Bus ☐ Train ☐ Bike ☐ Walk ☐
>   Reason _____
>
> 4) How do you travel to the shops?
>   Car ☐ Bus ☐ Train ☐ Bike ☐ Walk ☐

Travelling in London

Interpretation

1 Use the diagrams to answer the following questions.

a How many underground lines are there in London?

b Why do you think Londoners call the underground 'the tube'?

c Which tube line is named after a famous British queen?

d Does the tube cover only central London?

e If you need to catch a flight from Heathrow Terminal 4, can you get there by tube?

f Does the tube go under the River Thames?

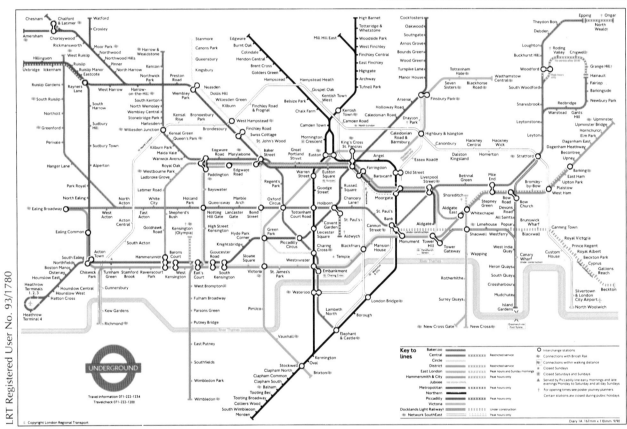

Using the London Underground

2 You are a tourist in London and you are at Oxford Circus.

a Which line should you take to get to
i) Green Park ii) Marble Arch iii) Regents Park?

b If you travel from Oxford Circus to the following stations, where do you change?

Example:

To Knightsbridge   *Change at Green Park*
To Goodge Street
To Sloane Square
To St Paul's

c In which direction would you travel from Oxford Circus to the following stations?
The first one is done for you.

STATION	DIRECTION
Charing Cross	Northbound
Queensway	Eastbound
Victoria	Southbound
Holborn	Westbound
Euston	

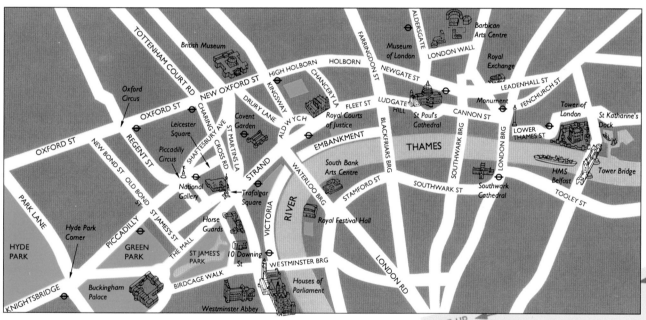

Sightseeing quiz

3 Match these famous sights on the map to the descriptions.

Buckingham Palace	The Prime Minister lives here.
The Tower of London	The Queen lives here.
Houses of Parliament	Charles and Diana got married here.
10 Downing Street	The Crown Jewels are kept here.
St Paul's Cathedral	The political parties meet here.

Tourist game

4 Plan a sightseeing trip around London for one day. Plan to visit no more than four places and have a picnic lunch in a park. Start your trip at Oxford Circus station at 9am. Make a note of each place you will visit, the tube line you will take and the station where you will get out. Use all the maps to help you. Finish your day at the Rock Garden hamburger restaurant in Covent Garden.

The future

Pre-reading

1 **a** What is the Channel?

    b Why are there three tunnels?

    c Why was the Tunnel link an historic occasion?

    Describe what is happening in the photograph.

What a day!

The Channel Tunnel

The stretch of water which separates Britain from France and the rest of mainland Europe has always played a significant role in British history. Saturday, 1st December 1990 was no ordinary day in the Channel's long history. At 11.00 a.m. two miners, one French and one English, cut through the last few centimetres of chalk separating the UK from mainland Europe. It was the first land connection since the Ice Age!

Work began on Eurotunnel in 1987. It is also known as the Channel Tunnel, the Chunnel or Trans Manche link. It was built by an Anglo-French engineering company, Eurotunnel, across 34 km of water from Cheriton (near Folkestone in SE England) to Coquelles (near Calais in NW France). A smaller central service tunnel was built to be used by workers and engineers for maintenance work and emergencies. The two outer tunnels will carry high-speed passenger and freight trains. Cars and lorries are also transported by train.

The tunnel is expected to have a positive effect on British industry and will no doubt boost the tourist industry. Journeys between Britain and Europe will be quicker and more reliable for both holidaymakers and businesspeople.

Lorry drivers will be able to relax and enjoy their shorter Channel crossing. Only one question remains. With the sea no longer acting as a natural barrier, will swimmers continue to try to swim the Channel as they have done for years?

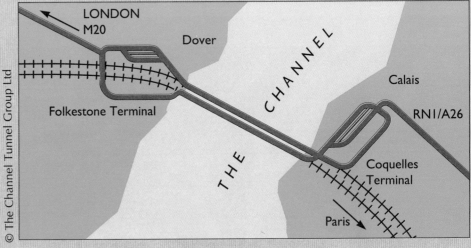

© The Channel Tunnel Group Ltd

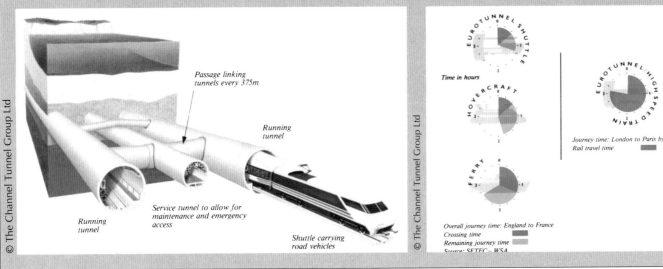

© The Channel Tunnel Group Ltd

Passage linking tunnels every 375m

Running tunnel

Running tunnel

Service tunnel to allow for maintenance and emergency access

Shuttle carrying road vehicles

Time in hours

EUROTUNNEL SHUTTLE

HOVERCRAFT

FERRY

EUROTUNNEL HIGH SPEED TRAIN

Journey time: London to Paris by rail
Rail travel time

Overall journey time: England to France
Crossing time
Remaining journey time
Source: SETEC – WSA

2 **a** List all the advantages of the Tunnel. Can you think of any more?

    b Calculate the journey time from your home town to Paris and on to London (including the Channel Tunnel link!).

    c Compare Eurotunnel with a Hovercraft crossing. How much time is saved? Why do you think this is?

FACT FILE

Driving in Britain

- Vehicles drive on the left.
- The speed limits are:
  Built-up areas = 30 mph (48 kph)
  Single carriageway roads = 60 mph (97 kph)
  Motorways = 70 mph (113 kph)
- Wearing a seat belt in the front seats of a car has been compulsory since 1983.
  In 1989 it became law for children under 14 to wear seat belts in the rear seats. Since July 1991 seat belts must also be worn by adults in rear seats – this applies to taxis as well as cars.
- People can take a driving test at 17 years and over.
- A British driving licence is valid until the driver's 70th birthday.
- Unleaded petrol is cheaper than leaded petrol, to encourage drivers to use it. The British are concerned about damage to the environment.
- Most petrol stations (garages) are self-service.
- Over 65% of British households have the use of one or more cars.

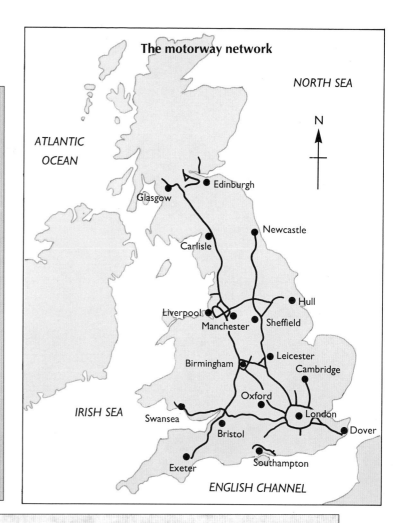

The motorway network

The London Underground

- It was the first city underground system in the world.
- It is more than 130 years old; construction started in 1860.
- You can hear the sound of trains and feel movements in many London flats and houses.
- 2.8 million journeys are made every day.
- There was a 70% increase in passengers in the late 1980s.
- The underground links Heathrow Airport with the centre of London.
- The most recent line, the Jubilee, was named to commemorate Queen Elizabeth's Silver Jubilee (25 years on the throne) in 1977.

- The underground saved the lives of thousands of Londoners during World War II (1939-1945). People slept on the platforms during bomb attacks at night.

Cards and celebrations

Greetings cards

Pre-reading

1 **a** Choose a card for your
   - mother
   - brother
   - best friend

   b Which card would you give if someone
   - is ill?
   - is about to take their driving test?
   - is moving house?
   - has got a new job?

2 **Match these inside messages (greetings) with the cards above.**

A *Sending you all my love on Valentine's Day*

B *With best wishes for your future*

C *Wishing you every success!*

D *Hope you have a very happy birthday*

E *With lots of love on your special day*

F *Hoping you'll soon be well again*

G *Wishing you every happiness in your new home*

3 **Do people send cards to each other in your country?**

Look at the list opposite. Put a tick (✔) next to the occasions when you would send a card.

Occasions and celebrations – When do the British send cards?

☐ birthdays
☐ Christmas
☐ Easter
☐ Valentine's Day (14 February)
☐ Mother's Day
☐ to say 'Thank you' to someone
☐ wedding anniversaries (the date someone got married)
☐ when someone passes an exam
☐ when someone passes a driving test
☐ when someone gets married (or, in recent years, engaged)
☐ when someone has a baby

Cards, hundreds of cards!

The card industry

Sending cards is a widespread custom in Britain today. The British have been sending cards since Victorian times when wealthy families started to send Christmas greetings. In the 1980s the card industry rapidly expanded as celebrations became more and more commercialised. There are cards for every occasion from buying a house to having a baby and, more recently, cards for getting a new job, getting a divorce or just saying 'Sorry'. More than 100 million Christmas cards are sold in Britain every year. However, cards are no longer confined to special celebrations such as birthdays, because there are many less important occasions when people send cards to each other.

Cards at school and at work

In some schools the giving of Christmas cards can be very organised, with a school postbox for pupils to post their cards to friends and teachers. In primary schools the teacher may display pupils' birthday cards in the classroom on their special day. When a teacher leaves the school or gets married the whole class will buy a card and everyone signs it. It is also customary at work to receive cards from the whole office on a special occasion. When people retire, they usually receive a big card from all their colleagues to wish them a happy retirement.

Keeping in touch

Card-giving is also widespread amongst people who do not know each other well or who do not see each other often. Cards are sent at Christmas as a way of 'keeping in touch' with past friends as well as relatives who live in other parts of the country. Companies produce a company card to send to all their important customers and some hotels send cards to previous guests.

Cards last for ever

People like to decorate their homes at Christmas by hanging the cards on the wall. Birthday cards are often displayed on a table or shelf for everyone to see and read. Special cards are kept for future years, to look at and remember, like looking through an album of old photographs. Cards, in many ways, have taken over from the letter. Even if you do not have time to write a letter, you can send a little card!

Reading comprehension

4 **a** When did card buying start in Britain?

b Why have card sales increased in the last twenty years?

c Can you send a card to someone who is not a relative or close friend?

d What do the British do with the cards they receive?

e Cards were originally intended for special occasions. What would you describe as a special occasion in your country?

f Which would you prefer to send, a card or a letter?

g Some people think that card-giving has become an obsession in Britain. Do you agree?

Look at the Fact File on page 49 for more ways to greet British people.

Customs and habits

Pre-reading

1 **Match these descriptions to the pictures above.**

a eating lunch in the street
b opening a door for someone
c queuing for a bus/in a shop
d shaking hands

e smoking in public/during a meal
f giving up a seat on a bus
g kissing a person you meet
h hugging a person you meet

2 **What are the customs in your country? Tick (✔) the appropriate box.**

a What do you do when you meet a stranger?

☐ kiss
☐ bow
☐ shake hands

Do you do the same when you meet an old friend or a member of your family?

b Do you give up your seat on a bus or train in your country? If so, who for?

☐ children
☐ old people
☐ pregnant women

c Do you queue for things in your country? When?

☐ in shops
☐ for buses
☐ for tickets

VISITORS TO BRITAIN are often surprised by the strange behaviour of the inhabitants. One of the worst mistakes is to get on a bus without waiting your turn in the queue. The other people in the queue will probably complain loudly! Drivers in cars can become quite aggressive if they think you are jumping the queue in a traffic jam. People respond to queue-jumping in an emotional way. Newspaper headlines describe anger at people who pay to bypass a hospital waiting list to get an operation more quickly. Queuing is a national habit and it is considered polite or good manners to wait your turn.

In recent years smoking has received a lot of bad publicity, and fewer British people now smoke. Many companies have banned smoking from their offices and canteens. It is becoming less and less acceptable to smoke in a public place. Smoking is now banned on the London Underground, in cinemas and theatres and most buses, and there are special smokers' carriages on trains. It is considered rude – or bad manners – to smoke in someone's house without asking 'Do you mind if I smoke?'. Public attitudes are reflected in 'Lonely Hearts' columns, where people advertise for non-smoking partners, and in advertisements for flats or houses to rent.

On the other hand, in some countries it is considered bad manners to eat in the street, whereas in Britain it is common to see people having a snack whilst walking down the road, especially at lunchtime. Britons may be surprised to see young children in restaurants in the evenings because children are not usually taken out to restaurants late at night and, if they make a noise in public or in a restaurant, it is considered very rude. In Victorian times it used to be said that 'Children should be seen and not heard', since children did not participate at all in public life. In recent years children are playing a more active role and they are now accepted in many pubs and restaurants.

Good and bad manners make up the social rules of a country and are not always easy to learn because they are often not written down in books! These rules may also change as the society develops; for example, women did not go into pubs at the beginning of this century because it was not considered respectable behaviour for a woman. Now both women and men drink freely in pubs and women are fully integrated into public life.

We may think that someone from a different country is being rude when their behaviour would be perfectly innocent in their own country. Social rules are an important part of our culture as they are passed down through history. The British have an expression for following these 'unwritten rules': 'When in Rome, do as the Romans do'. Do you have a similar expression in your country? Have any of your social customs changed since your grandparents were born?

Interpretation

3 a Look at the pictures in Exercise 1. One of the situations is often considered rude. Which one?
   b Find two habits which have changed in Britain during this century.
   c **Answer TRUE or FALSE.**
      i   Britons complain about queuing.
      ii   Smoking is not allowed on the London Underground.
      iii Eating in the street in Britain is acceptable behaviour.
      iv   Children should not make a noise in a restaurant.

   d Complete this table, using the text and the pictures in Exercise 1. Make notes.

   Are there any habits that you share with the British? Tick (✔) the British habits that you find unusual.

Polite	Good manners in Britain	Good manners in my country
Rude	Bad manners in Britain	Bad manners in my country

45

Parents and society – free choice?

Pre-reading

1 Our rights are based on the rules of our society and differ from country to country. Many rights depend on your age and are decided by law. Other rules are decided by your parents. Are parents strict in your country?

Do your parents allow you to...?

	YES	NO
Drink alcohol		
Smoke		
Stay out all night		
Have friends to sleep at your house		
Hold a party at home		

How old do you have to be to ...?

vote in an election

get married

leave school

drive a car

buy alcohol

Young voices, old problems

In the age of Aids, raves, video, and crack, streetwise teenagers' views of life and parents still seem familiar

ANDREA, 13, from Finchley, north-west London: My mum let me out on my own when I was about 10 – I could go anywhere really, as long as I let her know. I always had to be back by about 7 pm. My mum will slap me across the face if I am rude to her.

KIRSTY, aged 17, from York: I think years ago there were so many restrictions and my mum was brought up really badly. She's 37 now. She was not allowed to go anywhere or do anything, which is why she got married at 16, just to get away. I go to nightclubs and pubs, even though I shouldn't. My mum likes me to be in by about one o'clock in the morning and she never goes to sleep before I am in. She doesn't say I have to be in by then, but I am.

HANNAH, 14, Golders Green, north-west London: When I was eight I was allowed out on my own as long as it was not far and my parents knew where I was. Normally I was allowed to stay out until dark. My parents have never hit me. If I am naughty they sit me down and explain why I was wrong and ask why I did it.

CLAIRE, 16, from Goole: I am an only child so I am spoilt. I don't really feel I have any restrictions at all. As far as drugs or real drinking is concerned, my mum knows I would never do anything like that anyway. She trusts me and I do not let her down. I will definitely be stricter. I get away with murder but my kids will not.

ALISON, aged 16, from Bath: I'm going out tonight to a club and it will be 3 am before I get in. I have just finished my GCSEs so my parents won't mind so long as they know I'm catching a taxi home and what time I will be in. I started going to clubs when I was 14. Sometimes I used to get into arguments with my parents about. Although I've been going in pubs since I was 14, I don't drink a lot.

JEREMY, 16, from Glasgow: I think I've had a clear sense of what's right and wrong since I was 10. I've been living with an older cousin and his wife for the past year. There are rules, like during the week when there's school, in bed by 12, no smoking in the flat. I think I'm a lot harder on myself now than I was when I was younger.

Source: *Independent on Sunday,* 4 August 1991

Reading activity

2 Read these extracts from interviews with teenagers in Britain for National Opinion Polls in 1991. Write one sentence for each person to describe what they can or cannot (are allowed/ not allowed to) do.

Interpretation

3 **a** Who has the strictest parents in your opinion?
   b Do these teenagers have to be home later or earlier than you?
   c Do you think it is dangerous to allow ten-year-olds out on their own without an adult?

KEY WORDS	THE GENERATION GAP
conflict generation gap parents	Since the 1950s teenage views of life and parents' opinions have been in **conflict**, a difference which is often called the **generation gap**. Teenagers in Britain today still say 'Our **parents** don't understand us'.
teenagers independence leave home growing up	By comparison with young people in other industrialised nations, British **teenagers** have a great deal of **independence**. Schools, the media and young people themselves place a lot of importance on being independent. Many teenagers have Saturday jobs and lively social lives, and most students over 18 live and study away from home. Young people even **leave home** to share a flat with friends and this is considered a positive sign of independence. Financial independence is also an important part of **growing up**, especially after the age of 18.
youth discussion	In the early 1990s Channel Four television featured a series of **youth** discussions in a programme called *Crosstalk*. The presenters, the audience and the viewers were teenagers and the programme motto was 'No parents allowed'. The most popular topics for **discussion** (chosen by British teenagers) were: part-time jobs, exam stress, parents' reactions to boyfriends or girlfriends, television programmes for young people, divorce and leaving home.
protective 'grown up' law	British parents would like to be **protective** until their children reach 16 but it seems that young Britons want to be '**grown up**' as early as possible. Over half the 14–16-year-olds in Britain already go to nightclubs and pubs for an alcoholic drink even though this is against the **law**.

What do parents think?

4 Use the text and these diagrams showing the results of national surveys in Britain in 1991 to answer the questions.

a At what age are most children left on their own at home?
b At what age do parents allow most children to go out alone?
c Do parents have the same rules for boys and girls?
d How many young people live away from home?
e How do these figures compare with your country? Do British parents give more or less freedom to their children than parents you know?

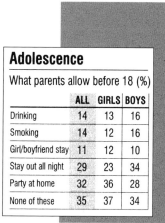

Adolescence
What parents allow before 18 (%)

	ALL	GIRLS	BOYS
Drinking	14	13	16
Smoking	14	12	16
Girl/boyfriend stay	11	12	10
Stay out all night	29	23	34
Party at home	32	36	28
None of these	35	37	34

Source: *Independent on Sunday,*
4 August 1991

Flying the nest
Percentage of 15 to 24 year-olds who don't live with their parents

Denmark	Britain	The Netherlands	Germany	France	Portugal	Greece	Belgium	Ireland	Spain	Luxembourg	Italy
52	37	35	33	25	23	22	21	15	14	10	9

Source: Politiken

Source: *Guardian,*
1 February 1991

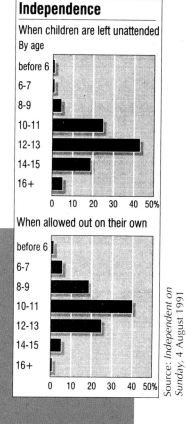

Independence
When children are left unattended
By age

before 6
6-7
8-9
10-11
12-13
14-15
16+

0 10 20 30 40 50%

When allowed out on their own

before 6
6-7
8-9
10-11
12-13
14-15
16+

0 10 20 30 40 50%

Source: *Independent on Sunday,* 4 August 1991

FACT FILE ACTIVITIES

Speaking

1 a Interview your partner.
Make notes.

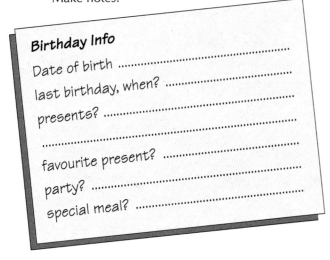

Birthday Info

Date of birth ....

last birthday, when? ....

presents? ....

....

favourite present? ....

party? ....

special meal? ....

b Make notes for
your country.

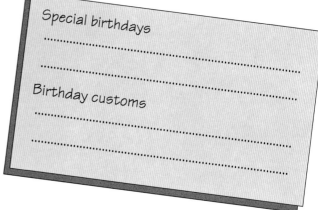

Special birthdays

....

....

Birthday customs

....

....

Writing

2 a Write a message for the following:
a card for a cousin who is getting married
a card for your best friend's birthday
a card for your parents' wedding anniversary
a card for a friend in hospital

Reading

3 a Compile a list of 'social rules' to help someone visiting your country.

b In recent years smoking has come to be regarded as socially unacceptable in Britain.
Are there any practices which are considered antisocial in your country?

Rights

4 a Match each of these
questions from an
information leaflet for British
teenagers to the section to
which you think it belongs.

QUESTIONS
When can I leave home?
Can my parents make me go to the school
they want?
Can my teacher hit me?
When can I open a bank account?
When can I get a job?
When can I start drinking alcohol?
When can I get married?

b Try to answer the
questions without
looking at the Fact File
opposite. Are the
answers the same for
your country?

SECTION
You and your parents
Relationships
You and school
You and the law
Money and work

FACT FILE

1 Celebrations

'Happy Birthday!'
Birthdays are a special occasion for British people.
Did you know ......?

☐ The following birthdays are often celebrated with an extra-special card and often a party:
1st, 18th, 21st, 30th, 40th, 50th, 60th

☐ A *hundredth* birthday is the most special. Everyone who reaches the age of 100 receives a telegram with birthday greetings from the Queen.

☐ Organised parties for children are very popular. You can have a party at a fast food-restaurant (e.g. Macdonalds, Pizza Hut) or in a discotheque, leisure centre or even in a castle!

2 Greetings

Here are some useful phrases for cards or the end of a letter:-

Congratulations on	your new baby
	passing your driving test/exam
	your new job
	finding your dream home
Wishing you	a Happy New Year
	a Happy Birthday
	every happiness in your life together
	many more years of health and happiness
Hope you	get well soon
	have a lovely holiday

3 Social rules

Did you know?

► It is polite to ask someone you know 'How are you?' when you meet them again, or at the start of a phone conversation. The expected reply is 'Fine, thanks' or 'Not too bad, thank you' – not a full health report! Strangers usually do not talk to each other on trains.

► It is polite to open a present in front of the person who gives it to you.

► It is polite to ask permission to leave the table after a meal, especially in the case of children.

► It is not polite to make telephone calls in other people's houses, unless you ask permission and offer to pay for the call.

► People do not take off their shoes when they enter a house.

► It is not polite to stare (look closely) at strangers.

► Children are expected to give up their seat on a bus to an adult, if the bus is full.

4 Rights

Many of our rights depend on what age we are. These include:

Age	Right
Birth	have a bank or building society account
5	compulsory school attendance
7	draw money from your own post office, bank or building society account
10	be convicted of a criminal offence
12	buy a pet without a parent being present
13	take a part-time job, up to 2 hours a day (after school and on Sundays) and up to 4 hours a day on Saturdays and in school holidays
15	own an air rifle
	be fingerprinted
16	leave school
	buy cigarettes
	hold a motorcycle licence
	marry with parents' consent
17	hold a motor car licence
	be sent to prison
18	marry without parents' consent
	buy alcohol in a public house
	vote at elections
	sit on a jury
	buy goods on hire-purchase
	place a bet in a betting shop
21	stand as a candidate for Parliament or the local council
	supervise a learner driver
	hold a Heavy Goods Vehicle licence
	adopt a child

Food and drink

Meals

Pre-reading

1 **What do you know about British food and drink?**

a Name one popular British dish ....

b Name one popular British drink ....

c Name one popular British snack... .

Now read and check your answers.

MEALS IN BRITAIN

The Health Education Authority asked a number of people in Britain what sort of meals and snacks they eat regularly. Here are the most common replies to the survey.

BREAKFAST

The most popular choices are:
a bowl of cornflakes and a cup of tea
a bowl of muesli and fresh orange juice
a piece of toast with marmalade
a yoghurt and fresh fruit with black coffee or tea.

The traditional British breakfast is a cooked meal of bacon, eggs and sausages, preceded by cereal or fruit and followed by toast. Nowadays, this large meal is served mainly in hotels and is very popular with foreign visitors. Britons may eat this big breakfast at weekends or on special occasions but prefer a smaller, healthier meal to start a normal day.

SNACKS AND LUNCHES

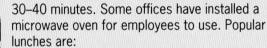

Lunch is a light meal and is eaten at school or work. Lunch takes 30–40 minutes. Some offices have installed a microwave oven for employees to use. Popular lunches are:
a salad or a sandwich
a baked potato
beans on toast.

Snacks are very popular in Britain and many people frequently eat snacks between meals. Schools and workplaces may also sell snacks such as crisps, chocolate, sweets and biscuits. Instant snacks are the fastest-growing sector of the food market; 5.5 million packets of crisps are sold every year. British kids eat more sweets than any other nationality. Biscuits, chocolates and sweets worth more than £5 billion were sold in Britain in 1990.

DINNER AND TAKE-AWAYS

Dinner is usually the main meal of the day and consists of two courses – meat or fish and vegetables followed by a dessert or pudding. Pre-packed or pre-cooked convenience foods are especially popular. £3,000 million of frozen foods are sold in an average year. Sixty per cent of British homes use a microwave oven for cooking.

In recent years, foreign foods have become a regular part of the British diet. Indian, Italian and Chinese dishes are particularly popular for evening meals. Most supermarkets sell a range of pre-packed meals to be heated in the microwave.

Take-aways became extremely popular in the 1980s. The traditional British take-away is fish and chips eaten with salt and vinegar and served in an old newspaper. Most towns and cities now offer a wide range of take-away meals, from American-style hamburgers to Turkish kebabs. Many families prefer to eat take-away food for dinner instead of cooking, and it is not unknown for people to buy a take-away after a visit to the pub or after a night out – in addition to dinner!

The British are famous for their love of sweet things, and afternoon tea with sandwiches, scones, jam and several different kinds of cake was once a traditional custom. Like the English cooked breakfast, it is now more often found in teashops and hotels than in private homes, and you can buy special guidebooks to tell you where the best afternoon teas are served. Most working people do not have tea as an afternoon 'meal', but they do have a short break in the middle of the afternoon for a cup of tea. Tea is often also drunk with lunch and dinner.

Reading comprehension

2 Are the following statements TRUE or FALSE according to the text?

a Most people have a large breakfast.
b Lunch is a light meal.
c Dinner is smaller than lunch.
d Frozen food is not popular.
e Everything stops at teatime.
f Tea is a drink and a meal.

Writing

3 Write a paragraph describing the meals and 'typical' food in your country.

Changing habits

FIBRE

FAT

SUGAR

Pre-reading

1 **a** List the names of as many foods and drinks as you can find in the pictures.

b Do people in your family or your country eat a lot of any of these foods? Which ones?

CHANGING HABITS – THE NUTRITION REVOLUTION

1 Since the 1970s eating habits in Britain have undergone a change. People have been encouraged by doctors, health experts and government advertisements to eat less fat and more fibre. Fat is believed to be one of the major causes of obesity and heart disease. Forty per cent of adults in Britain are overweight, and Britain has one of the highest death rates due to cardiovascular disease in the world. High fibre foods and low fat foods can now be found in all shops and supermarkets.

2 Britons have also become more aware of calories, the energy value of food. Some people count the number of calories they eat every day, so that they can try to take in fewer calories and lose weight. This is called a calorie-controlled diet. Manufacturers are increasingly producing special foods with fewer calories for slimmers. One of the fastest-growing sectors of the food market in Britain today is slimming foods.

3 Food manufacturers have started to help the general public to make more informed choices about what they eat. Most food packaging gives information about the content of the food, and the ingredients are listed by law. This sophisticated information service has made British people more aware of what they are putting in their mouths.

---

2 **Match each of these headings to the correct paragraphs in the text above.**

   a The slimming boom
   b Public information
   c The fat and fibre story

Reading activity

3 **a** Name two types of food that the British are eating more and less of respectively.
   b Choose two of the foods illustrated which you think contain a lot of calories. Check your ideas with your class.
   c Why do some British people count calories?
   d Study the nutritional information label. Is the product good for you or bad for you in large quantities?

Vocabulary – Shopping bag adjectives

4 Study the pictures of supermarket food above. Which adjectives or words do the manufacturers use to tell you that the food is 'good for you' (e.g. pure juice)?

NUTRITIONAL INFORMATION		
Average Values:	Per 100 g	Per 850 g Can
Energy	315 kj (73 kcal)	2677 kj (620 kcal)
Protein	4.9 g	41.7 g
Carbohydrate	14.0 g	119.0 g
Fibre	7.3 g	62.1 g
Fat	0.2 g	1.8 g

School food

Pre-reading

1 a Make a list of the foods that you think are 'healthy'.

b Read the school canteen menu and tick (✔) any foods that people eat in your country.

c Some of the dishes on the menu have come to Britain from other countries. Which ones?

Match these popular meals to their country of origin.

curry	Spain
pizza	Greece
spaghetti bolognese	India
shish kebab	Mexico
chicken chow mein	Italy
moussaka	Turkey
chilli con carne	USA
paella	China/Hong Kong
hamburger	Italy

d You are going to eat at Chapel Park Middle School today. You can have a main course, a vegetable course, a dessert and a drink. Underline the ones you would choose.

Speaking

2

Healthy Eating

1 How often do you skip a main meal or eat alone?
a   Often
b   Sometimes
c   Almost never

2   How would you estimate your intake of fruit and vegetables yesterday (include potatoes)?
a   Hardly any at all
b   2 or 3 portions
c   4 or more portions

3   How many times in a week would you eat "meats" such as pork pies, burgers, luncheon meat, or meat pies?
a   Not very often, maybe once or twice
b   Five to eight
c   A lot more than nine

4   Did you eat three fibre-rich foods yesterday (eg wholemeal bread, nuts, breakfast cereal, baked beans, root vegetables like carrots, parsnips, beetroot, sweetcorn, or jacket potato)?
a   No
b   Maybe one or two
c   Yes

5   How many times a week would you have an alcoholic drink?
a   Most days
b   Perhaps once
c   Do not drink alcohol

6   How many times a week do you have a fried meal (eg egg and bacon or fish and chips)?
a   Less than four

b   Five to eight times
c   Over eight

7   Which of these best describes your lunchbox?
a   Mostly crisps, some form of chocolate bar, biscuits or cake
b   It usually has at least one of these foods – yoghurt, apple or some kind of fruit, a raw vegetable like a carrot
c   It's made up almost totally of foods listed in (b) above

8   Find the fat! Which food in each of these three pairs has the most fat?
a   Meat pie or potato
b   Hard cheese (such as cheddar) or cottage cheese
c   Packet of salted peanuts or 10 tomatoes

ANSWERS
Q1: a1, b2, c3.   Q2: a1, b2, c3.
Q3: a3, b2, c1.   Q4: a1, b2, c1.
Q5: a1, b2, c3.   Q6: a3, b2, c1.
Q7: a1, b2, c3.
Q8: One point for each of the following: a meat pie, b hard cheese, c salted peanuts

Over 18 points: you seem to eat a healthy diet
12–17 points: room for improvement in your diet
under 12: your diet could be storing up health problems for your future.

Source: *Early Times*, 18–24 July 1991

CITY CUISINE

Social and Welfare Catering Division Menu for Chapel Park Middle School, Friday, June 28

Spaghetti Bolognese
Fish Bite
Chicken and Savoury Rice
Assorted Quiches
Stuffed Jacket Potato
Ploughmans Lunch

Garlic Bread
Boiled Potatoes
Creamed Potatoes
Chips

Spring Cabbage
Carrots
Beanshoots
Baked Beans

Side Salad
Pasta Salad
Beetroot
Apple and Celery Salad

Trifle
Gingerbread
Assorted Biscuits
Ice Cream and Wafers
Cheese and Crackers
Fresh Fruit
Yoghurt

Orange Juice
Milk
Tea
Cocoa

Newcastle Evening Chronicle, 2 July 1991

Writing

3 a Write a short description of what you ate yesterday. Make notes before you start and include:

size of meal
when you ate it
where you ate it
types of drink/snacks.

b Keep a diary in English of everything you eat this week. At the end of the week read your diary – you may get some surprises!

SEASIDE ROCK & A CHOCOLATE MILKSHAKE

4 a List the food and drink mentioned in the interviews under the following categories: FAT FIBRE SUGAR

b Which is the healthier, Niall's breakfast or Adrian's breakfast?

c Name two things eaten by Niall or Adrian which are definitely *not* good for you. What could they eat instead?

d Do Niall and Adrian eat more or less than you?

NIALL FOLEY, 13, OF LONDON: 'For breakfast I had two slices of buttered toast, with white bread – white toast is better than brown – and a cup of tea with pasteurised milk and two sugars.

For lunch I had chips, cheeseburger, carrots and a biscuit, with milk to drink. Lunches at my school are quite good. We have quite a good selection – lots of curries, lasagne, and pizzas.

As soon as I got in I had an apple and a drink of orange squash. For tea I had a chocolate bar and a packet of crisps. Then we had ham salad, followed by fruit cocktail with cream.'

Niall had an orange squash with his tea. He generally has a sandwich and an orange squash before going to bed, then takes another drink of squash or water up to bed.

ADRIAN JARRETT, 8, OF CHESHIRE: 'I had Rice Krispies for breakfast with semi-skimmed milk – no sugar today – and a glass of milk. For break I had a banana.

My packed lunch was cheese spread sandwiches, with brown bread, a banana yogurt, a packet of bacon crisps, and blackcurrant juice in a flask. I don't like school lunches, and I prefer white bread.

For tea I had tinned spaghetti with toast and orange squash. I had a Fab ice lolly. I'm going to have supper – seaside rock and a glass of chocolate milkshake!'

Source: Early Times, 18–24 July 1991

5 **Write a short description of this photo. Use these questions to help you.**

Who is in the picture?
Why are they eating together?
Are they enjoying themselves?
What types of food are they eating?
What time of day is it?
Is it healthy food?
What are the children thinking?
What are they planning to do after the meal?

Time, gentlemen, please!

Pre-reading

1 Describe this picture.

a Who are the people?
b Where are they?
c What time of day might it be?
d What are they drinking?
e Are there similar places in your town or country?

PUBS IN BRITAIN

Pubs (public houses) can be found in every town, city or village. Social life for many people has centred on the pub for many years. Opening and closing times are decided by law (pubs in England and Wales close at 11 p.m.) and ten minutes before closing time the barman or barmaid rings a bell or shouts, 'Last orders!'. When you go into a pub you have to go to the bar, pay for your drink and carry it to your seat.

It is customary in Britain to 'go for a drink' with friends. People often meet at a pub before going on to another place. On Friday and Saturday evenings pubs in some city centres can be very crowded. Some people do a tour of all the pubs in one area and have a drink in each one; this is called a 'pub crawl'. It is usual for each person in a group to take it in turns to buy drinks for everyone, and this is called a 'round'. Pubs often also provide entertainment: live music, singing, juke boxes and, more recently, computer games, video and karaoke machines.

It used to be difficult to get a cup of coffee in a pub, and children were not allowed inside. Although it is still against the law to serve alcohol to anyone under 18, pubs are now trying to encourage families. Pub meals have become very popular over the past ten years and are generally cheap and often good. Pubs with gardens or chairs and tables outside are often crowded in the summer. Pubs are still a central part of British culture. It is no surprise that two of Britain's favourite TV soap operas have a pub as their focal point, *Coronation Street* (the 'Rover's Return') and *East Enders* (the 'Old Vic'). In both of these TV programmes you will see a popular game called darts, which is often played as a team game in pubs throughout Britain.

A Timely Reminder!

THIS PUB'S OPENING HOURS ARE

MONDAY	11 30	2·30 5·30 11 00
TUESDAY	11 30	2·30 5·30 11 00
WEDNESDAY	11 30	2·30 5·30 11 00
THURSDAY	11·30	2·30 5·30 11 00
FRIDAY	11·30	11·00
SATURDAY	11·30	11·00
SUNDAY	12·00	2·30 7 00 10·3

Beer or wine? It depends on where you live

Litres per person, 1985

150 — 125 — 100 — 75 — 50 — 25 —

UK WEST GERMANY FRANCE PORTUGAL ITALY

Of these countries, West Germany has the highest consumption of spirits at about 8 litres a year, Portugal the lowest at 2 litres.

Reading comprehension

2 a What are the busiest times for pubs?

b Do you have to drink alcohol in a pub?

c What team game is played in a pub?

d Who serves you in a pub?

e What time is last orders?

f What is a 'round'?

g Can you have lunch in a pub?

Interpretation

3 a These cartoons come from a government book which describes two social problems in Britain today. What do you think they are? Do you have similar problems in your country?

b Look at the Contents page. In which section do you think you would find each of the two cartoons ?

Contents

Writing activity

4 Write a reply to this letter which appeared in a teenage magazine in Britain. Try to give practical suggestions to help the writer.

I THINK I'M AN ALCOHOLIC

I really need your help. I think I am an alcoholic. I'm 17 and I have to have a drink every night or I don't sleep. I go out with friends on Fridays and get very drunk. I've tried to stop going out, but people say 'oh, go on' and I end up going out.

I wake up before school needing a drink. I'm doing 'A' Levels and my work is suffering because I'm always thinking about drink so I can't concentrate.

I'm always broke from buying drinks and I've started stealing money from my family to buy it. I need help, so please print this letter. I'm suicidal and I will not phone Alcoholics Anonymous because I'm too scared. Please help.

The media

The press

Pre-reading

1 **What are your reading habits?**

    a Do people in your family read newspapers?

    b How often do you read newspapers?

    c What's the most popular newspaper in your class?

    d Do you know the names of any British newspapers?

2 **Tick (✔) TRUE or FALSE before you read.**

                                                    T F

    a British people read a lot of newspapers. □ □

    b Papers are owned by political parties. □ □

    c People read more papers on Sundays. □ □

    d All papers are printed in black and white. □ □

Now read and check your answers.

KEY WORDS	NEWSPAPERS IN BRITAIN
	If you get on a bus or catch a train in Britain, especially during the morning and evening 'rush hour', when most people travel to and from work, you will see a lot of
national	people with their heads in a newspaper. More daily newspapers, **national** and
regional	**regional**, are sold in Britain than in most other developed countries. On an average
morning	day two out of three people over the age of 15 read a national **morning** paper;
Sunday	about three out of four read a **Sunday** paper. There are about 135 **daily** papers and
daily	Sunday papers, 2,000 weekly papers and nearly 100 papers produced by members of
	ethnic minorities (60 of which are Asian papers). A lot of people buy a morning
evening	paper, an **evening** paper and a couple of Sunday papers so it is not surprising to
circulation	learn that national newspapers have a **circulation** of 15.8 million copies on
	weekdays and 17.9 million on Sundays.

The press caters for a variety of political views, interests and levels of education.

'quality'
popular
tabloid

colour

Papers are generally divided into **'quality'** papers which are serious with long, informative articles, and **'popular'** papers known as tabloids because of their smaller size. **Tabloids** are less serious and contain more human interest stories than news. In the 1980s a new quality paper, *The Independent*, and a new tabloid, *Today*, were introduced. *Today* had pictures and pages in **colour** and that started a fashion; now most tabloids are in colour.

independent
political party

leader

Newspapers are almost always financially **independent** of any **political party**. Nevertheless, during general election campaigns many papers recommend their readers to vote for a particular political party. The paper's editor usually writes an open letter called a **'leader'** to the readers.

ownership
publishing groups
Broadcasting Bill

Ownership of the national, London and regional daily newspapers is concentrated in the hands of large press **publishing groups**. In the early 1990s the government's **Broadcasting Bill** aimed to pass laws to prevent too much media ownership being in the hands of one individual or organisation.

What's the mystery word?

3 Use the text and clues to complete this puzzle about the press in Britain.

CLUES (Down)
1 A new 'popular' paper
2 The number of copies sold
3 The papers are not usually financed by these.
4 You read this type of paper at the end of a week.
5 Papers that are read all over the country
6 These are serious papers.
7 You buy this paper on your way home from work.
8 These people are in charge of the papers and write 'leaders'.
9 *Today* is one of these.

What's the mystery word?

Inside a newspaper

4 Where would you find an article about …?

- a tennis match
- the situation in the Middle East
- temperatures in Scotland today
- a film premiere in London
- the Queen's speech in Parliament
- a Summit meeting in Strasbourg
- movements on the Stock Market

Inside

Arts, Reviews	17
British News	7–10
Cartoons	23
Crosswords	23, 24
European News	5
Financial News	11–13
Guardian Society	15
Law Guardian	18
Letters	2
Obituary	23
Sports News	20–22
Women	16
TV, Radio and Weather	23
World News	4, 6

Periodicals

5 There are 7,000 periodicals in Britain and they are classified as 'consumer general interest', 'special interest' and 'business to business'. General and special interest magazines cover a very wide range of interests. Here are three of the most popular:

The Radio Times
Woman's Own
Smash Hits

Try to guess

a what they are about;
b what type of people read them.

Look at the covers and choose a magazine for someone you know. Give reasons for your choice.

BBC 1

5.35pm
Neighbours
Todd and Josh believe they may know the identity of a murderer. What action should they take? The truce between Paul and Glen doesn't last very long.

6.00pm
Six O'Clock News
With Anna Ford and Andrew Harvey.
Weather Penny Tranter

6.30pm
Regional news magazines

7.00pm
Eldorado
Snowy urges a distraught Bunny to go and find Fizz. Trish receives a mysterious invitation from Olive.

7.30pm
Liverpool in Europe
Liverpool v Apollon Limassol
Live, uninterrupted coverage of the whole of this European Cup Winners' Cup first-round, first-leg match.

9.30pm Main News
With Martyn Lewis.
Regional News
Weather Penny Tranter

10.00pm
Inside Story
Investigative documentaries.
The Women Trade
Hidden cameras expose a cruel 'flesh trade' in which thousands of women from poor countries are lured to Europe for jobs that turn out to be in the sex industry.

10.50pm
The Breakfast Club
FILM John Hughes's witty and emotional comedy drama featuring early performances by some of the 'brat pack' and starring **Emilio Estevez**
Five total strangers with nothing in common – a swot, a beauty, an athlete, a rebel and a recluse – are thrown together when they have to spend the whole of one Saturday in high school detention. Before the day is over, they will break all the rules, bare their souls and find true friendship in the unlikeliest of places.
12.25-12.30am Weather

2.15-2.45am
BBC Select
Accountancy Television:
Business Account – a preview of the new weekly technical update and training programme for accountants.

3.15-4.00am
BBC Select
TV Edits: another chance to record a preview of new resources for advanced students in French and German.

BBC 2

5.30pm
Inside the Russia House
A film about four advertising students from Newcastle upon Tyne who travelled last year to the former Soviet Union.

6.00pm
Star Trek
The cult 1960s series, starring **William Shatner Leonard Nimoy**
The Naked Time. Spock and Tormelon land on Psi 2000 to evacuate a team of scientists only to find them all dead. *(Rpt)*

6.50-7.40pm
DEF II
Wayne's World
More excellent fun from the noisiest basement in Aurora, Illinois. Join Wayne, Garth and a celebrity guest partying on down.

7.00pm Teenage Diaries
Programmes made by young people about their own lives.
The Daughter Sent from Hell
Jennifer is 15 and desperately wants to be 'a normal teenage girl', but she lives with her mother who is severely disabled with multiple sclerosis. Frustrated by having to be a carer instead of care-free like her friends, Jennifer uses her diary to try to come to terms with her dilemma.

7.40pm
The Shetland Sessions
Aly Bain travels north to the island of Yell in tonight's programme from the 1991 Shetland Folk Festival.

8.10pm
The Un-Americans
To Hell with Truth. The dilemma of whether to name names dominates the final part of this *Timewatch* documentary on the 'red scare' in postwar America. Witness Harvey Matusow, an ex-communist, at one stage testified that 126 'reds' were working for the Sunday *New York Times* when only 96 people worked on the paper. Yet for a time no one questioned his lies. His fame and fortune are contrasted with the experiences of those who refused to co-operate. In destroying some, but trusting others, did America lose faith in its most basic values?

9.00pm ScreenPlay:
A Little Bit of Lippy
An outrageous northern comedy film by Martyn Hesford, winner of the *Radio Times* Drama Award for *A Small Mourning.*
Starring **Kenneth Cranham Rachel Davies**
When 19-year-old Marian Fairley finds a pair of women's knickers in her husband's laundry, she takes the TV, the microwave and the baby, and moves in down the road with her parents. But an even bigger shock awaits her.

10.10pm
ScreenPlay Firsts
Short graduate films.
Supper at Emmaus
An art historian teaches a class of students in front of Caravaggio's masterpiece. With Raad Rawi, Hannah King and Julia Tarnoki.

10.30pm Newsnight
Presented by Jeremy Paxman.

11.15pm The Late Show
Late-night arts magazine.

11.55pm Weatherview

12.00-12.55am
Open University
Social Scientists at Work

ITV

5.40pm
Early Evening News
With John Suchet.
Weather Martyn Davies

6.00pm
Regional news magazines

6.50pm
Coronation Street
Baby Duckworth sets about disrupting the normal peace and quiet of the Duckworth household.

7.10pm
The European Match
Stuttgart v Leeds United
Manchester United v Torpedo Moscow
A football double bill featuring league champions Leeds United and last season's runners-up Manchester United.

10.00pm
News at Ten
Alastair Stewart and Trevor McDonald with the latest national and international news.
Weather Martyn Davies
10.30pm Regional News and Weather

10.40pm
Obsession
FILM Suspense thriller starring **Cliff Robertson Genevieve Bujold**
When Michael Courtland's wife and daughter are kidnapped, the police advise him not to pay the ransom and assure him that they will help him get his family back. But plans backfire and his family are never seen again. Sixteen years later he meets a woman who is the double of his missing wife.

12.30am
Hollywood Report
American film news from a British point of view.

1.00am The Body Stealers
FILM Science-fiction adventure starring **George Sanders**
A former air force general investigates the disappearance of several parachutists and believes that it might be the work of aliens.

2.45am America's Top 10
The latest US chart sounds, pop videos, news and gossip.
(Repeated tomorrow at 4.30am)

3.15am Videofashion
Uptown New York. A look at the collections of some of New York's top designers, including Oscar De La Renta, Adrienne Vittadini and Caroline Herrera.
(Repeated tomorrow at 5.00am)

3.40am Quiz Night
Another round of the popular pub quiz. With Ted Robbins.

4.10am Grand Ole Opry
The world's oldest continuous running radio show is televised featuring many of country music's biggest stars such as Loretta Lynn, Barbara Mandrell, Roy Acuff, Ricky Skaggs and Larry Gatlin. *(Rpt)*

4.40am Fifty years On
Archive newsreel clips including the launch of the Iowa, Russian girls in the United States and the Battle of Britain anniversary. (Black and white)

5.00am Three's Company
American comedy series.
Itching for Trouble. A former high-school girlfriend of Jack's on whom he had a crush, moves to town and asks him to meet her. Jack is deflated to find out she is only seeking advice concerning her jealous husband. With Joyce De Witt, John Ritter, Priscilla Barnes, Richard Kline, Don Knotts and Don Sparks.

5.30-6.00am Morning News
Plus news reports throughout the night

CHANNEL 4

5.50pm
The Bunbury Tails
Animated adventures of a team of sporting rabbits.
Le Buns 24-Hour Race (Part 1) The Bunburys compete in a 24-hour motor race in France.

6.00pm
Treasure Hunt
Two competitors guide skyrunner Anneka Rice around Sussex. With Kenneth Kendall and Wincey Willis.

7.00pm
Channel 4 News
Presented by Jon Snow.
Followed by **Weather**

7.50pm Comment
Another personal view.

8.00pm
Brookside
Rod and Terry find themselves in competition.

8.30pm
Inspector Morse
The detective returns to solve the first of four murder cases. Starring **John Thaw Kevin Whateley**
The Infernal Serpent
A respectable academic family comes under the spotlight as Morse investigates the death of an eminent scientist.

10.30pm
Packing Them In
More backstage mayhem coupled with comedy and variety acts hosted by Jenny Eclair, Frank Skinner and Kevin Eldon. Tonight an abandoned baby is found in the theatre. With guests Lily Savage, Kinky Friedman and Avner the Eccentric.

11.15pm
Mojo Working
The last of the series profiles Jimi Hendrix, one of rock 'n' roll's greatest guitarists, and attempts to define the impact and importance of his music.

11.45pm
Marc Bolan – the Legendary Years
A 15th anniversary tribute to Marc Bolan, lead singer with T Rex, who died in a car crash on 16 September 1977. The programme includes rare music footage, conversations with Bolan himself, plus interviews with his widow June Field, Dave Hill and Jimmy Lea of Slade, Steve Priest of the Sweet, and Mickey Finn and Bill Legend of T Rex.

12.45am
The Steve Allen Show
American satirical comedy series from the 1950s hosted by Steve Allen. Tonight's guests include Sammy Davis Jr and Miss America of 1957.
(Black and white)

1.15-4.20am
Seeta aur Geeta
FILM The series of Hindi films continues with this action-packed saga. Two sisters choose different courses of action when confronted with the same situation – a date with destiny. A Hindi film with English subtitles. With Hema Malini, Dharmendra and Sanjeev Kumar.

Pre-reading

1 a Look quickly at the TV page opposite and answer the questions.
   i How many channels are there?
   ii What time does TV finish at night?

b Programmes in Britain are divided into categories. Find a programme for each category:

Light entertainment   Children's
   (includes variety shows/soap operas/   Music
   situation comedies/game shows)   Sport
News/current affairs   Films/TV movies
Documentaries   Drama/plays

What type of programme do you like best?

TELEVISION VIEWING IN BRITAIN

Television viewing is by far the most popular leisure pastime in Britain. Britons also call it 'watching the box' or 'the telly'. The average viewing time per person is just over 25 hours a week.

Britain is one of the world's foremost exporters of TV productions, which continue to win large numbers of international awards, especially for documentaries, nature programmes and drama serials.

Britain also buys programmes from abroad and in 1990 nearly half the programmes came from the USA. American soap operas like *Dallas* and *Dynasty* became very popular in the 1980s, as did detective series.

Recent years have seen the start of 'Youth TV' which aims to give programmes for young people. Children's TV has always been very active and includes shows made by young people. One of the oldest and most popular is *Blue Peter* on BBC 1.

THE CHANNELS

BBC 1
Broadcasting since 1936.
General interest programmes, light entertainment, sport, current affairs, children's programmes.

BBC 2
Covers minority and specialist interests as well as music, serious drama, travel programmes, documentaries, and foreign films in the original language.

ITV
33% informative (news, current affairs, documentaries and 66% light entertainment, sport, films.
Advertisements ('ads') are shown every 15 minutes.

CHANNEL 4
Began in 1982 and aims to appeal to the interests not catered for by ITV. It shows 15% educational programmes and encourages innovation and experiment. It has ads.

Adapted from *HMSO Britain 1991 Handbook*

---

2 Use the text to complete this chart for Britain.

	BRITAIN	YOUR COUNTRY
Number of channels		
Advertisements?		
Foreign programmes		
Average viewing hours		
Children's programmes		

3 Now fill in the chart for your country. How do your answers compare?

The video boom

Pre-reading

1 **Electronic media puzzle**

   a Complete this puzzle with the names of the objects in the pictures. The 'mystery word' is the name of an important object in many British homes. Use it to complete the title of the magazine article.

   b Have you got any of these things at home? Are they popular in your country?

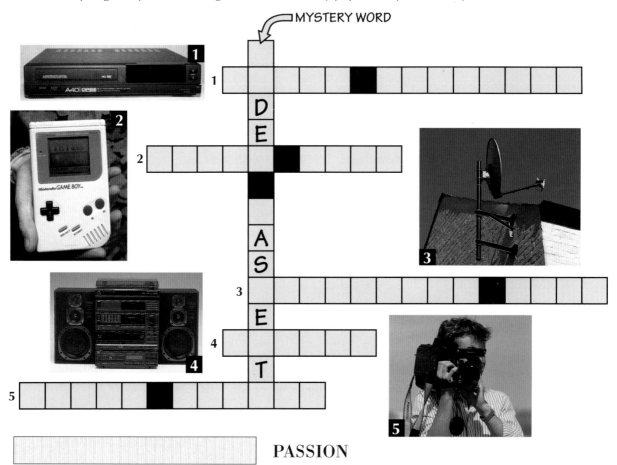

PASSION

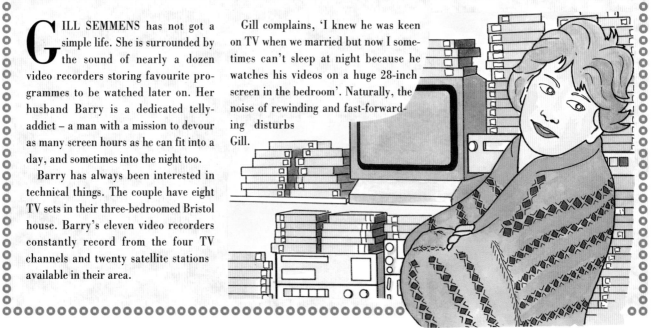

GILL SEMMENS has not got a simple life. She is surrounded by the sound of nearly a dozen video recorders storing favourite programmes to be watched later on. Her husband Barry is a dedicated telly-addict – a man with a mission to devour as many screen hours as he can fit into a day, and sometimes into the night too.

Barry has always been interested in technical things. The couple have eight TV sets in their three-bedroomed Bristol house. Barry's eleven video recorders constantly record from the four TV channels and twenty satellite stations available in their area.

Gill complains, 'I knew he was keen on TV when we married but now I sometimes can't sleep at night because he watches his videos on a huge 28-inch screen in the bedroom'. Naturally, the noise of rewinding and fast-forwarding disturbs Gill.

Barry defends himself: 'I'm very selective in my viewing. I like watching mainly documentaries, news and technical programmes'. He buys a TV guide, satellite magazines and the daily papers to make his careful selection of programmes to tape. He uses over 200 video tapes a month!

Barry explains, 'We don't think we are anti-social, we both have jobs where we meet a lot of people'. Nevertheless, Gill does admit that she takes a tiny hand-held TV to work. 'I love game shows, particularly American ones', she says.

Barry is particularly excited about his new satellite dish for the European satellites. 'I can honestly say that video recorders have revolutionised my life', states Barry proudly. Do you agree?

Adapted from *Woman*, 1 June 1992

Comprehension

2 a Read the article and find expressions which mean the same as:

cassette   television   choice   to be interested in   to consume   very small

b Does Barry think he is a TV addict?

c Does Gill agree completely with Barry's habits?

Writing

3 In pairs, make a list of the advantages and disadvantages of video recorders. Compare your ideas with your classmates.

Speaking – group decision-making

Programming a video recorder

4 **'An evening's viewing'**
You are going to use one of Barry's video recorders to tape programmes. Use the TV guide on page 60 to plan your recording in groups. Try to agree on programmes which everyone will want to watch later on.

VIDEO RECORDING SHEET

TIME	PROGRAMME

FACT FILE ACTIVITIES

Radio

1 **a** All radio stations have listeners. Match these people to the station you think they may listen to:

> a teenager   a 40-year-old man   a housewife   a politician
> a London taxi driver   a writer   a foreign student

b Make a chart to compare radio stations in your own area/country.

Newspapers

2 **a** Use the information in the table to make a comparison between 'quality' papers and 'popular' papers. This language will help you:

> smaller/larger   more serious/lighter   cheaper/more expensive
> the same as/different from

b Compare two papers in your own area/country.

64

FACT FILE

Radio stations

Popular with young listeners. Britain's main pop and rock station.

Mainly classical music, poetry, drama, short stories, news, cricket.

Pop, rock, jazz. Information on London transport/traffic-jams/events.

Broadcasts worldwide. Uses English and 35 other languages. English lessons are broadcast daily with explanations in 25 languages.

Popular with middle-aged listeners. A broad range of popular music and light entertainment.

News, drama, comedy, current affairs, documentaries. Parliamentary debates are broadcast live.

37 BBC local radio stations/ 70 other independent stations/ 300 hospital radios.

sport/education (new station)

The newspapers

| QUALITY PAPERS | POPULAR PAPERS |

The Daily Telegraph

The Guardian

THE TIMES

THE INDEPENDENT

INDEPENDENT ON SUNDAY

OBSERVER

FINANCIAL TIMES

SUNDAY TELEGRAPH

THE SUNDAY TIMES

The Mail ON SUNDAY

The Daily Star   Today

People   SUNDAY Mirror   Sunday People

NEWS OF THE WORLD   Sunday Express

THE Sun

DAILY Mirror   Daily Express

Daily Mail

'Broadsheets' – double the size of tabloids

Long articles, lots of words

A few diagrams and photos, less emphasis on visual

Formal/serious tone

Emphasis on national and international news and comment – aim to inform educated people about the world

Wide vocabulary and standard English

Average price 45p

Tabloid size (16" by 23")

Short articles in general

Very visual – lots of photos, illustrations, diagrams

Sensationalist – articles about scandals

Emphasis on mass entertainment as much as news, interest in TV soap operas, Hollywood stars, and Page 3 (nude) girls

Simple language, but sometimes difficult for foreigners due to use of slang, puns etc.

Average price 25p

Adapted from *Communication and Media Studies*, Macmillan 1988

Britain: A leisure society

Pre-reading

1 a Study the diagram and answer the questions.

   i What time do people usually start work? Finish work?

   ii How much time do they spend on eating meals?

   iii How much leisure time do they have?

b Now make comparisons for your own family/country.

Use:

> longer/shorter hours, earlier/later, less time/more time

c Copy the basic diagram and complete it for your family/country.

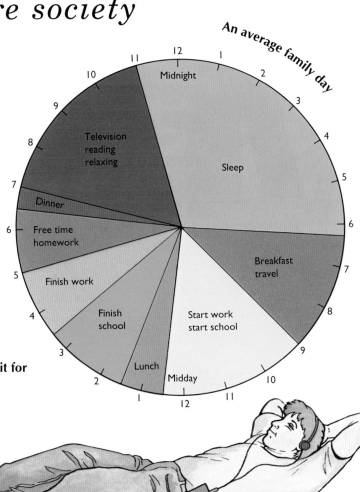

An average family day

d Before you read, make a list of the activities you associate with leisure (free time) e.g. dancing, reading, watching sport.

_____

_____

_____

_____

_____

_____

_____

_____

A LEISURE SOCIETY

Britain has in recent years been described as a 'leisure society'. This is because there is a greater variety of leisure pursuits and people have more spare time and money to spend on relaxation. Most spare time is spent at home after work or at the week-ends.

Young people generally go out on Friday or Saturday nights to a disco, to a concert or to the pub. Older people may go to the pub or to the theatre, or visit friends. In recent years going out for a meal or bringing a take-away meal home have become popular with all ages.

Sunday is traditionally a day of rest and town and city centres can be very quiet or even deserted. People read the Sunday newspapers, go for a walk in the park or countryside or work at home in the garden. A lot of people wash their cars on Sundays or do jobs around the house (DIY).

In the past, local authorities provided libraries, museums and parks for everyone. In the 1980s people became more interested in keep-ing fit and relaxing, so leisure services were expanded to include leisure centres, sports centres (20 in 1972 and 1,500 in 1987), health clubs and theme parks. Indoor pools, with their wave-making machines, water slides and tropical vegetation, have become very popular. Cinemas have been redesigned with four or more screens, each showing a different film at the same time. Naturally the leisure industry per-suades people to spend a lot of money, especially on new and more expen-sive interests such as computer games and sports equipment.

Interpretation

2

a Describe a typical Sunday in your country. Is there a 'Sunday atmosphere'? Does it differ from a British Sunday? If so, how?

b Where do young people in your town/city/village go for a night out?

c Study the chart. Tick the activities that people do in your family.

d Make a similar chart for your country. What is the most popular spare-time activity?

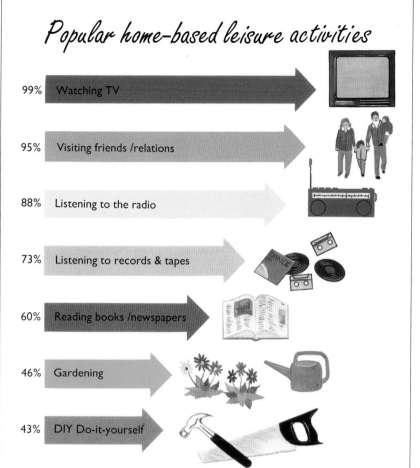

Popular home-based leisure activities

99% Watching TV

95% Visiting friends /relations

88% Listening to the radio

73% Listening to records & tapes

60% Reading books /newspapers

46% Gardening

43% DIY Do-it-yourself

Statistics based on *HMSO Social Trends 21*, 1991

3 Here are the results of a leisure survey conducted by the Scouts in Britain in 1991. As you read, match the survey questions to the conclusions in the article (number each question in the correct order).

Survey questions

☐ Are you a member of a youth group?

☐ Do you play with video games?

☐ How much time do you spend on video games?

☐ Do you prefer outdoor or indoor pursuits?

☐ Would you like to join a youth group?

☐ How many hours of TV do you watch per day?

☐ If you could take up (start) a new pastime, what would you do?

☐ What are your favourite hobbies/pastimes?

Use the questions to interview students in your class.

A SURVEY conducted for The Scouts has uncovered a gap between young people's aims of healthy, outdoor communal activity and the reality of what many actually do.

① The nationwide survey was conducted as part of an awareness campaign for the Scouts' £10 million Promise Appeal. This aims to boost membership, particularly in the inner cities and among ethnic minorities. The survey showed that 77 out of 100 of respondents preferred outdoor activities to staying indoors, with 84 saying they would like to join groups involved in outdoor activities.

② Despite this, the survey showed that young people are spending almost four hours each day in front of the television. Half of those questioned spend almost five hours a week playing video games.

Additionally, the survey reveals that:

③ ● Scouts and children belonging to other youth groups spend less time in front of the television than the average 11-16 year old

④ ● While swimming, football and cycling are among the most popular activities, the majority of respondents wanted to take part in more adventurous pastimes

⑤ ● Sixty out of every 100 questioned said they would like to go camping and 40 wanted to try rock climbing, canoeing or windsurfing

⑥ ● Sixty-three wanted to belong to a youth group

Source: *Early Times*, 7–13 February 1991

Sport in Britain

Sports vocabulary

SPORTS WORD SEARCH

```
g p y r d a g o l f
y t b u r t e g y o
m f c g s h h a m o
n e t b a l l y v t
a e d y r e z u l b
s f b x r t b y f a
t t e n n i s w c l
i z k h o c k e y l
c s q u a s h v p h
s w i m m i n g t b
```

1 **a** The photographs show some of the sports which are played in British schools. Can you find their names in the Word Square? Do you play the same sports in your school?

    b Can you find the names of any other sports in the square? Divide all the sports into the following categories:

Indoor sports	outdoor sports	racket sports	ball sports	team games

    c Can you add any more sports to your list?

Pre-reading

2 **a** Name two types of sports clothing.
   b Describe two ways of keeping fit.
   c Name two charities in your country.

KEY WORDS	THE RUNNING BOOM
fit healthy jogging participate	During the 1980s there was a great increase in interest in getting **fit** and staying **healthy**. A lot of people started running and **jogging** in their spare time. Aerobics classes opened in every town and the number of sports centres for the community increased to 2,000 with 1,700 indoor recreation centres. The four national Sports Councils in England, Scotland, Wales and Northern Ireland launched a campaign in 1987 called *What's your sport?*, designed to encourage people to take an interest and **participate** in sport. Children are also encouraged to be physically active and most schools have a gymnasium or a sports hall for dance and movement.
sports clothes fashionable designer big business	In the 1980s lots of new and colourful **sports clothes** started to be sold in shops. It is now **fashionable** to mix ordinary clothes with sports gear (training shoes/tracksuits) to relax in at home or even to wear out. You can wear a **designer** sweatshirt to go skateboarding or to just look good at a disco. The money to be made from the sale of 'designer' sportswear is **big business** in the 1990s.
London Marathon sponsored run Sport Aid worldwide	The **London Marathon**, thanks to TV coverage in the 1980s, has become an internationally famous event. The sight of so many runners competing has encouraged many Britons to 'have a go'. There are now over 100 marathons every year in Britain and many towns organise **sponsored runs** or walks to raise money for charity. The international charity project **Sport Aid**, started by the Irish rock star Bob Geldof, organises a **worldwide** sponsored run called 'The Race Against Time' to help raise money for the starving in Africa.

Reading comprehension

3 **a** Why was there a running boom in Britain?
   b What were the aims of the Sports Councils' 1987 campaign?
   c When do people wear sports clothes?
   d Why did marathons become popular?
   e Are sports clothes regarded as fashionable leisurewear in your country?

Activity

4 Despite the increase in the numbers of people participating in sport, the majority of Britons still prefer to be spectators. Watching sport on TV is a popular leisure activity, as is going to football matches on Saturday.

Study the TV page in Unit 8, page 60.

   a Make a list of all the sports you can find.
   b How many channels show sports programmes?
   c Is there a sports channel?

The changing nature of British holiday habits

Pre-reading

1 a **Answer the questions about your family holidays.**
  - Where do you usually go for your family holidays?
  - Where did your grandparents use to go for their holidays?
  - How many weeks' holiday do you and your parents get per year?
  - How many weeks' holiday did your grandparents use to get?

b Look at your answers to the above questions. Are there any differences or similarities? Can you explain them?

	1951	1960	1971	1985	1987	1991
Holidays abroad (in millions)	1.5	3.5	7	16	20	20
Total Holidays	26.5	35	41	49	75	54

Interpretation

2 a **Tick (✔) the sentences which best describe the diagram:**
  - ☐ British people are taking fewer holidays than in 1951.
  - ☐ More Britons started to go abroad in the 1960s.
  - ☐ More people are taking holidays now than in 1951.
  - ☐ Fewer people go abroad than in 1951.
  - ☐ A lot more Britons started going abroad in the 1980s.

b What do you notice about the figures for 1991? Can you think of a reason for this?

c Write a short description of holiday habits in your country.

Pre-reading

3 **People go abroad for many reasons. Tick (✔) the reasons which seem most likely to you.**

People don't like Britain any more.
Holidays in Britain are more expensive than abroad.
People prefer a foreign climate.
There are not enough hotels in Britain.
Britons are richer now so they can afford foreign holidays.
Transport facilities have improved (airports/ferries).
There are more foreign holidays on sale in travel agencies.
Britons have a longer holiday entitlement than before.
The beaches in Britain are very polluted.

Now read and check. Were you right? What are the main reasons?

KEY WORDS	WHY GO ABROAD?
	The past 25 years have seen the most dramatic change in holiday habits. The British are
affluence	going abroad, including ordinary families. A combination of growing **affluence** and rapid
mass transport	**mass transport** means that a lot of people can afford a two-week holiday in the sun.
technology	Improvements in airline **technology** mean that plane tickets are cheaper, planes can
charter flights	carry more people and **charter flights** are constantly expanding.
package	Tour operators put together **'package'** holidays (including plane ticket, accommodation
boom	and meals) to Spain in the 1960s and there was a British tourist **boom**! Tour operators
	book a whole plane and fill it with holidaymakers. As the date of departure gets closer
	they become more and more anxious to fill the plane so they lower the price of the
	package. If you go to a travel agent in Britain you can buy a 'last minute' package, or a
	package holiday that someone`has cancelled, for up to 50% less than the original cost.
bargains	Travel agents' windows are full of **bargains**, particularly during the summer months.
destinations	Today there are many kinds of package holiday and lots of different **destinations**. The
	sea, sun and sand in the summer months is still the most popular choice but in the
	1980s winter skiing packages also became popular. In recent years there has been a
fashion	**fashion** for time-sharing, rented villa holidays and trips to faraway places like China,
luxury holidays	India or the West Indies. However, these **luxury holidays** are still sold mainly to middle-
	class Britons whilst the average holidaymaker still prefers the less expensive
Mediterranean	**Mediterranean** package. Spain, Greece and Turkey or Portugal are still the favourite
	destinations of most British tourists abroad, with trips to Florida becoming more frequent
	too. If you ask a lot of tourists why they go, they will often mention the unreliable British
weather	**weather** as the main reason. A lot of tourists are prepared to put up with long delays
tan	and queues at airports to get a few rays of sunshine and a **tan** to show off at home!

Reading comprehension

4 Match the beginning of each sentence with the correct completion, using *because.*

a There was a British tourist boom in Spain

b Package holidays are cheaper

c Tickets bought near the time of departure are often cheaper

d British tourists say they go abroad rather than stay in Britain

1 the climate in Britain is unreliable (it rains!).

2 tour operators started package holidays.

3 they include return plane tickets, hotels and meals.

4 the tour operator needs to fill up his plane.

Speaking/writing

5 a Design a class questionnaire to find out about holiday habits.
Include questions to find out:

length of stay   activities on holiday
holiday destination   type of accommodation
method of transport   reasons for holiday choice

b Describe your dream holiday. Where would you go? How would you get there? Who would you go with?

c Write a composition called 'Holiday trends in my country'. Try to include a contrast between holidays in the past and holiday habits today.

FACT FILE ACTIVITIES

1 a What type of place is popular with visitors to Britain?
Why do you think this is?

b Where can you ... see a Shakespeare play?
visit a Roman theatre?
go boating on a river?
windsurf on a lake?
visit a castle?
walk around the city walls?

c Make a list of the places that foreign tourists visit in your country.
Are they similar to Britain's favourite tourist spots?

Leisure

2 a Use the table to write a short summary to explain British leisure habits.

b Make a list of all the items that you or your family buy that could be considered leisure items (for pleasure and relaxing).

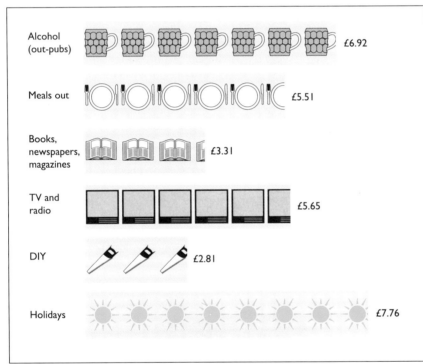

Alcohol (out-pubs)	£6.92
Meals out	£5.51
Books, newspapers, magazines	£3.31
TV and radio	£5.65
DIY	£2.81
Holidays	£7.76

Sport

THE BRITISH SPORTING CALENDAR

Summer
Cricket season
Wimbledon fortnight
Racing at Royal Ascot

Autumn
Soccer and rugby seasons begin
Horse of the Year Show
Braemar Royal Highland
    Gathering

Winter
Skiing season begins in
    Scottish Highlands
Fishing season starts in Scotland

Spring
End of soccer season – FA Cup
    Final
The Grand National horse race
The London Marathon
The Oxford and Cambridge
    University boat race on the
    River Thames

3 Write out a sporting calendar for visitors to your country.

Britons' favourite holiday destinations

1) Spain
2) France
3) Greece
4) The USA
5) Austria
6) Switzerland

Holidays

4 a Have you ever visited one of the countries in the list? Which one would you choose for your next holiday?

b Make a list of the favourite holiday destinations of people you know at home. Do they go abroad or stay in your country?

FACT FILE

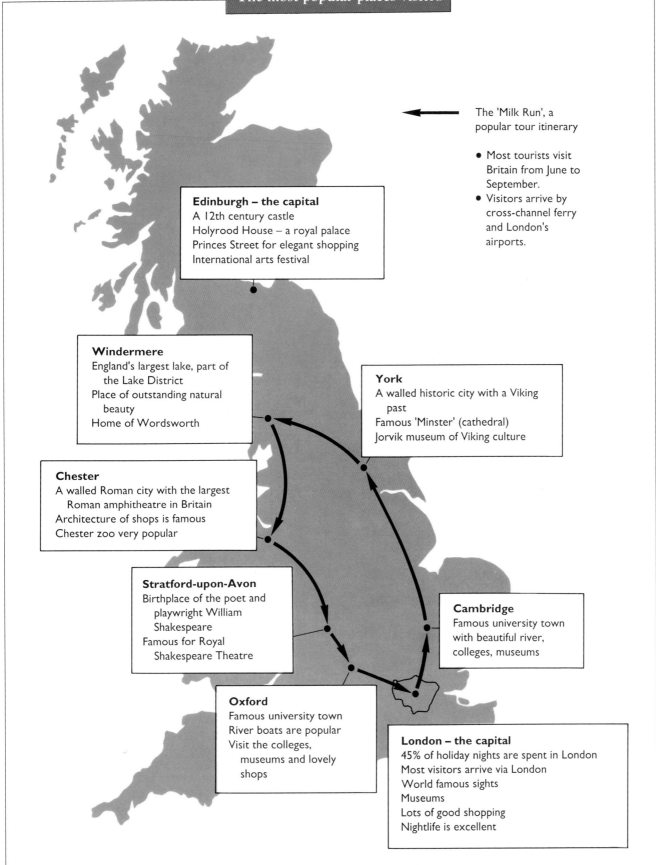

Overseas visitors to Britain
The most popular places visited

← The 'Milk Run', a popular tour itinerary

- Most tourists visit Britain from June to September.
- Visitors arrive by cross-channel ferry and London's airports.

Edinburgh – the capital
A 12th century castle
Holyrood House – a royal palace
Princes Street for elegant shopping
International arts festival

Windermere
England's largest lake, part of the Lake District
Place of outstanding natural beauty
Home of Wordsworth

York
A walled historic city with a Viking past
Famous 'Minster' (cathedral)
Jorvik museum of Viking culture

Chester
A walled Roman city with the largest Roman amphitheatre in Britain
Architecture of shops is famous
Chester zoo very popular

Stratford-upon-Avon
Birthplace of the poet and playwright William Shakespeare
Famous for Royal Shakespeare Theatre

Cambridge
Famous university town with beautiful river, colleges, museums

Oxford
Famous university town
River boats are popular
Visit the colleges, museums and lovely shops

London – the capital
45% of holiday nights are spent in London
Most visitors arrive via London
World famous sights
Museums
Lots of good shopping
Nightlife is excellent

Youth culture – teenagers

Pre-reading

1 Until the Second World War there was no transition period between childhood and adulthood in British society. Young people were called children until they were about 16 or when they started work, and then they became adults. Young people and their parents often shared similar clothes, attitudes and social life. Teenagers did not exist at the beginning of the twentieth century.

   a At what age are you considered an adult in your country?
   b Do you wear the same type of clothes as your parents?
   c Look up the word 'teenager' in a dictionary.
      Is there an equivalent expression in your language?
   d Why do you think the teenage years are called a 'transition period'?

2 Before you read, look at these photos and describe what you see.
Who are the people? Where are they? What are they doing?
When do you think the photos were taken?

The Birth of the Teenager

❶ After the war Britain's birthrate was the highest it had been since 1880. By 1959 there were over four million single persons between the ages of 13 to 25 because of this baby boom. Gradually these young people started to enjoy special status. The post-war economic recovery meant that people had more money to spend on luxuries and there were lots of jobs for young people. The young and single usually lived at home and could spend their wages on enjoyment. The working week was shorter than ever before, so there was more leisure time for all.

❷ Young Britons in the 50s looked to America for taste in fashion, hairstyles and music. Post-war Britain was quite an austere place and the glamorous movie-star images from the States, as well as the rebellious new sounds of rock 'n' roll, attracted young people.

Record shops, coffee bars and melody bars (playing music) appeared in towns. Dance halls full of young people in the latest American-style fashions provided exciting new places for the young to meet. These adolescents started to dress differently from their parents and even started to speak differently, inventing their own slang expressions to use amongst friends. Some of these new teenagers formed groups or gangs; the most famous were the Teddy Boys, all sharing the same style of clothes and attitudes. At first adults in Britain responded in horror, complaining that these new forms of dress, behaviour and speech were 'immoral' or 'a disgrace'.

❸ By the late 1950s the fashion and music industries had responded to the new teenage demand for records, transistor radios, fashionable clothes, posters of their idols and magazines about young people. Teenagers, because of their sheer numbers, were important consumers with money to spend. In the early 60s the London fashion scene became internationally famous. One of the London designers, Mary Quant, is famous for inventing the mini-skirt which caused quite a scandal at the time. Teenagers wanted to wear daring and colourful designs and the designers recognised this need and produced a 'look' at an affordable price.

❹ In 1962 the record 'Love Me Do' by an unknown group called The Beatles entered the American-dominated British record charts. It was the start of an important era for British music and many groups followed the success of the Beatles, such as The Who, The Rolling Stones etc. These years contributed to the popularity of British pop music worldwide and many musicians today were influenced by the work of John Lennon, Paul McCartney and other singer/songwriters of the era.

❺ The new heroes of teenage Britons in the 60s were often ordinary working-class youngsters who rose to fame as pop stars, fashion designers, photographers, writers or models. This phenomenon contributed to the confidence of British youth and gradually teenagers began to develop their belief in the right to choose their own clothes, lifestyle and attitudes towards politics, religion or sex. In 1939 the concept of the teenager did not exist in British culture but by 1959 teenagers had become an important part of society. It comes as no surprise that the late 50s and the early 60s are remembered in Britain as important years, to look back on with nostalgia.

3 Read and match these headings to the appropriate paragraph.

(A) Rock around the clock — paragraph …
(B) Trendy gear — paragraph …
(C) Baby boom — paragraph …
(D) Working-class heroes — paragraph …
(E) John, Paul, George and Ringo — paragraph …

Reading comprehension

4 Read the text again and answer the questions.

a Why were there so many young people in Britain in 1959?
b Which country influenced young Britons most in the 1950s?
c Why did young people have more 'spending power' in 50s and 60s Britain?
d Which industries benefited from the birth of the teenager? Why?
e Why were the Beatles so important at the time?
f Look back at the photos in Exercise 2. Can you say any more about them?

Writing

5 Read the text again.

Make a list of the three main factors which influenced the birth of the teenager in Britain. Expand your notes into a short summary.

Speaking – group decision-making

6 'Teenage time capsule'

You and your group are going to bury a box in the ground for future generations to discover in 100 years. This box should contain five objects which will tell the young people of the future as much as possible about life for teenagers in your country now. What would you put in your box? Decide together and describe your objects to the rest of your class. Try to explain why they are important. What do they tell you?

Spending habits

Pre-reading

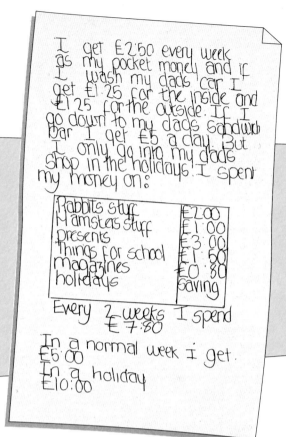

I get £2.50 every week
as my pocket money and if
I wash my dads car I
get £1.25 for the inside and
£1.25 for the outside. If I
go down to my dads sandwich
bar I get £5 a day. But
I only go into my dads
shop in the holidays. I spent
my money on:

Rabbits stuff	£2.00
Hamsters stuff	£1.00
Presents	£3.00
Things for school	£1.50
magazines	£0.80
holidays	saving

Every 2 weeks I spend
£7.80

In a normal week I get.
£5.00
In a holiday
£10.00

1 **a** Does Eva get pocket money? What
does she spend
her money on?

b Does she save a lot?

c Does she have a job?

d How much did Eva spend last month?

e How much is the total in your
currency? Is it a lot?

Reading activity

2 **a** Look at the graph and the article. They reflect two
aspects of teenage life in Britain. What are they?

b Compare your spending habits with those of British
teenagers. Are there any differences or similarities?
Does anything surprise you?

c It is illegal (i.e. against the law) to employ a child
under the age of 13 in Britain. Children over 13 often
have a Saturday job, e.g. helping out in a shop, or a
paper round on weekdays before school starts.
Do children have jobs in your country? Are there laws
in your country against the exploitation of children?

EXPLOITED SCHOOLCHILDREN

A survey conducted in the Nottingham
area has revealed that thousands of
schoolchildren are working illegally in
England.

One pupil, who is preparing for
GCSEs, works through the night at a sock
factory and then goes straight to the
classroom. At one primary school, 15
children aged between nine and eleven
were working illegally.

Source: The Indy No. 70, 31 Jan. 1991

Percentage of children spending pocket money on selected items, United Kingdom, 1990

- Crisps, sweets, ice cream
- Whatever I want
- Savings
- Comics, magazines
- Records, tapes
- Toys
- Books, stationery

Percentages: 0 20 40 60 80 100

Source: Wall's Pocket Money Monitor

Discussion

3 **Here are some common arguments for and against
teenagers working. Which ones do you agree
with? What do other students in your class think?**

- A job teaches young people the value of work.
- A job distracts youngsters from their studies.
- No child should be allowed to work, it's cruel.
- All children should have some work
experience before they go out into the 'real
world'.
- Saturday jobs help parents financially because
the kids earn their own money.
- If children have to work it means their parents
are too mean to give them enough to spend.

Pre-reading

4 **Match these words to the illustrations:**
cash/cash card/cash card machine (dispenser)/bank account statement/cheque book.

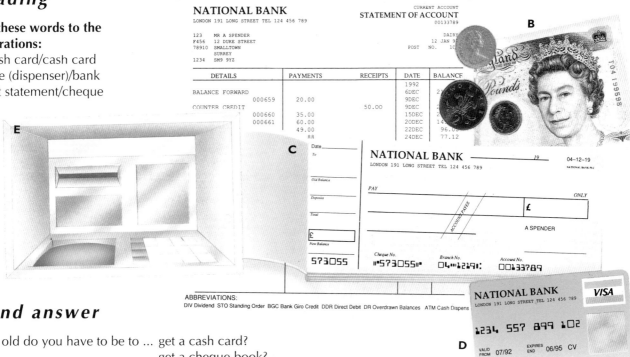

Read and answer

5 **a** How old do you have to be to ... get a cash card?
get a cheque book?
b What's the difference between pocket money and an allowance?
c What are the two main advantages of a cash card for teenagers?

MONEY AND YOU
Help your kids to spend wisely

Cash card schemes are available for anyone over the age of 13. So if your youngster's moved on from pocket money to a monthly allowance or if he now earns a wage, then he should think about opening his own account.

Not only are our children more knowledgeable about financial matters, but they are also far more eager to control their own affairs, according to a recent survey by the Britannia Building Society. In fact most teenagers would rather have a monthly allowance than the traditional weekly sum of pocket money. They want money in an account that they can control and budget with as they please.

A monthly allowance is usually the next step up from pocket money and frequently includes cash spent on essential expenses such as bus fares and school dinner money, as well as on new clothes and any other extras.

But children are only allowed a cheque book when they reach the age of 16. Until then cash cards, which in general are available on savings accounts for those over 13, seem to be a sensible option, and are now being offered by most banks and building societies.

Opening a cash card account gives teenagers many advantages. They learn to control their own finances, and the machine won't let them spend more than they have, which means they have to budget carefully. They'll also have easy access to their money in case of an emergency, for example, when a late night taxi is needed after the last bus home has gone.

For a time most cash card accounts were only available at building societies, for instance Prime Gold at the Woolwich and Cardcash at the Halifax. But now banks have also begun to offer accounts which are specifically aimed at teenagers.

These accounts are primarily card-operated current accounts, but also pay interest and privileges are added as the account holder gets older.

For example a 13-year-old who opens one of these accounts will not only get a cashcard but can advance to a cheque book when he reaches 16. Initially they offer no overdraft facilities, but are good at adapting to your child's different financial needs as he grows older. They include Lloyds Bank's Headway account, which offers interest starting at six per cent, as does Natwest's Card Plus. ■ Jean Stern

> **How much pocket money?**
> ● The Halifax Building Society suggests the average pocket money for 12-16 year olds is £3.60 a week.
> ● Research shows that 53% of all 16 year olds are earning - average wages are £9.24 for girls and £8.49 for boys.

Swop you two cash cards and my champion conker for your Gold card!

Next week: how to place a bet on a race

Source: *Best*, Issue 21/91, 30 May 1991

Interpretation

6 **a** Which would you prefer, an allowance or pocket money?
b Do young people have bank accounts in your country?
c Do you think it is a good idea to allow teenagers to handle their own money?

77

Music

Pre-reading

1 a Group the words in the box under the following headings.

A MUSICAL INSTRUMENT   MUSIC EQUIPMENT   TYPE OF MUSIC

reggae soul drums violin piano disco rock heavy metal tapes guitar
personal stereo records compact disc rap classical jazz folk house
saxophone bass

b Name – a British singer ....

a British group ....

a British record/song ....

c Complete this chart.

Number 1 this week	
Number 1 last week	
The fastest mover (up)	
A new entry	

TOP TWENTY

Last week's positions in brackets

1	(2)	Gypsy Woman	CRYSTAL WATERS
2	(3)	Promise Me	BEVERLEY CRAVEN
3	(1)	Shoop Shoop Song	CHER
4	(8)	Tainted Love '91	SOFT CELL
5	(—)	I Wanna Sex You Up	COLOUR ME BADD
6	(4)	Touch Me	CATHY DENNIS
7	(—)	Shiny Happy People	REM
8	(20)	Baby Baby	AMY GRANT
9	(15)	Call It What You Want	NEW KIDS ON THE BLOCK
10	(5)	Last Train To Trancentral	KLF
11	(7)	Fading Like A Flower	ROXETTE
12	(18)	Success	DANII MINOGUE
13	(6)	Sailing On The Seven Seas	OMD
14	(19)	RSVP	JASON DONOVAN
15	(—)	Caught In My Shadow	WONDER STUFF
16	(11)	Anasthasia	T99
17	(—)	Headlong	QUEEN
18	(—)	Your Swaying Arms	DEACON BLUE
19	(9)	Future Love Paradise	SEAL
20	(—)	Whenever You Need Me	T'PAU

Compiled for Metro Radio by MRIB

d Work in pairs.
Complete this questionnaire,
then ask your partner.

SMASH HITS readers survey

Favourite single ....

Favourite album (LP)* ....

Favourite singer ....

Favourite group ....

Favourite type of music ....

Favourite musical instrument ....

Number of records bought last year ....

*More CDs and cassettes are now sold in Britain than vinyl records.

Read and find out:

2 What is *Top of the Pops*?
When can you see it?
What type of people watch *Top of the Pops*?

TOP OF THE POPS

ew shows have a history as long as that of *TOTP*. It started in black and white in 1964. The first compere was Jimmy Savile. Among the stars he introduced on the opening night were the Beatles, the Rolling Stones and Cliff Richard. That was the decade when the capital was called 'Swinging London'.

In May 1983, more than nineteen years after its birth, *TOTP* celebrated one thousand performances. The programme has lasted because it reflects the ups and downs of the record charts and consequently the taste of the young people who buy the records.

Nowadays the charts are compiled by computer showing sales figures from selected record shops throughout the country. The results are published on Tuesday morning when the *TOTP* producer must decide which bands or solo artistes to include in the Thursday evening programme.

On programme day, a *TOTP* director is lucky if the schedule allows half an hour in which to rehearse a band. The show is mainly live performances and there's a carnival atmosphere. The audience is made up of young people between the ages of 16-24 who write to the BBC for a free ticket. *TOTP* is an important show for groups and singers since an appearance on the programme can mean instant stardom. It is also the show that British families most like to record on their video recorders.

The show ends with a run-down of the top 40 records that week in Britain and the famous last words of the DJ introduce the Number One single: 'It's Number One – it's Top of the Pops!'

Vocabulary

3 Find words in the text which mean the same as the following expressions:

a pop group - ....
the charts - ....
fame (to be famous) - ....
a TV presenter - ....
a singer - ....
a TV programme - ....

Speaking

4 Imagine you are a *Top of the Pops* producer. Make a list of four acts (groups or singers) you would include in a show. Then imagine that you are the presenter and introduce each performance.

Fashion in Britain

1960s

The 'Beatle' look
Mini-skirts
Unisex fashions
Psychedelic clothes
Flower power

1970s

Country look ('Laura Ashley')
Punk style
Glam rock

1980s

Sloane Ranger look
Designer labels
Sports clothes

1990s

Sports clothes
Sixties revival
Hippy revival
Rave style
Grunge

1 Match these sentences to the pictures.

   a Her formal, business clothes are more expensive than they appear.

   b This woman is not necessarily dressed for sport!

   c This teenager became one of the most famous women in the world.

   d They believed in peace and love, and adopted aspects of their dress from Eastern cultures.

   e This well-known rock star's clothes reflect his name.

   f She invented the mini-skirt in the early 60s.

   g This recycled fashion has lost much of its power to shock.

   h Their brightly-coloured hair and strange clothes have made them one of the tourist sights of London.

Source: *Fashion and Style*, Usborne

LONDON – THE FASHION CAPITAL

The British fashion scene is known for unorthodox clothes, with a young market and popular appeal. Recently, London has attracted a lot of international attention with its **designer collections** which are held at a hall called **Olympia**.

Vivienne Westwood is one of the pioneers of street style (the daring, youthful look which London is known for). Following in her wake and turning out fresh ideas consistently, are designers such as **John Galliano, Richmond Cornejo** and **English Eccentrics**. Other well-known names include **Zandra Rhodes** (fairytale clothes in original fabrics), **Katharine Hamnett** (slogan t-shirts and chic casuals) and **Bruce Oldfield** (glamorous evening wear).

British style: young, fresh and innovative

2 What's fashionable in your country at the moment?
What type of clothes do you like? (sporty/casual/smart/bright)
Which British fashion era most appeals to you?
Have you noticed anything unusual about 1990s trends in Britain?

3 **Which of these adjectives best describes British fashion today?**

> traditional   conservative   original
> old-fashioned   adventurous   boring

Writing

4 **In 1990 and 1991 a British high street bank, Lloyds, organised a fashion competition for teenagers in Britain. The bank asked young people to design suitable clothes for a famous person. The competition was very popular, and more than 15,000 teenagers sent designs. Now the competition is being repeated and you can try to win a designer T-shirt.**

The rules
Write a description of a suitable outfit to visit the following places:

a a visit to the bank manager

b a shopping trip to London

c a night out at a nightclub

Your famous person can be one of the following:

a a musician

b a politician

c a TV presenter

d a sports personality

11-18 YEAR OLDS · DESIGN AN OUTFIT FOR A CELEBRITY OF YOUR CHOICE

WIN THE FASHION

EXPERIENCE OF A LIFETIME WITH LLOYDS BANK

Lloyds Bank fashion challenge

Lloyds Bank

© Lloyds Bank Plc 1992

The British education system

Pre-reading

1 **Answer these questions for your own country.**

   a Do boys and girls go to the same schools?
   b Do you have to go to school by law?
   c At what age do children start school?
   d At what age can children leave school?
   e What type of education is there after school?

KEY WORDS	STATE EDUCATION IN BRITAIN
free	All state schools in Britain are **free**, and schools provide their pupils with books and equipment for their studies.
compulsory nursery	Nine million children attend 35,000 schools in Britain. Education is **compulsory** from 5-16 years. Parents can choose to send their children to a **nursery** school or a pre-school play group to prepare them for the start of compulsory education.
primary	Children start **primary** school at 5 and continue until they are 11. Most children are taught together, boys and girls in the same class.
comprehensive co-educational	At 11 most pupils go to secondary schools called **comprehensives** which accept a wide range of children from all backgrounds and religious and ethnic groups. Ninety per cent of secondary schools in England, Scotland and Wales are **co-educational**.
GCSE	At 16 pupils take a national exam called '**GCSE**' (General Certificate of Secondary Education) and then they can leave school if they wish. This is the end of compulsory education.
sixth form 'A' level	Some 16-year-olds continue their studies in the **sixth form** at school or at a sixth form college. The sixth form prepares pupils for a national exam called **'A' level** (Advanced Level) at 18. You need 'A' levels to enter a university.
further education	Other 16-year-olds choose to go a college of **further education** to study for more practical (vocational) diplomas relating to the world of work, such as hairdressing, typing or mechanics.
higher education degree graduate	Universities and colleges of **higher education** accept students with 'A' levels from 18. Students study for a **degree** which takes on average three years of full-time study. Most students **graduate** at 21 or 22 and are given their degree at a special graduation ceremony.

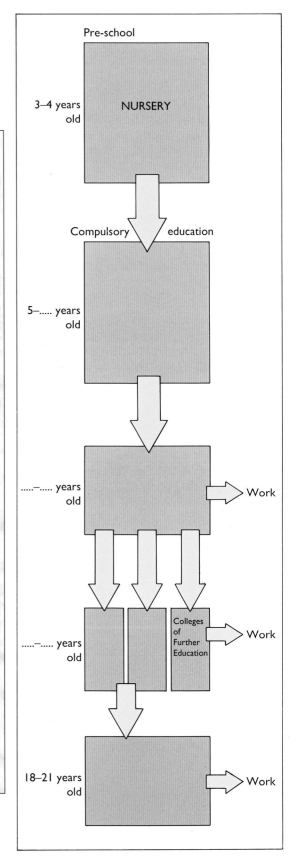

Reading activity

2 a Complete the diagram by writing the name of each type of school in the boxes. Write the age of pupils at each type of school.

b Match each of these words from the text with the correct definition.

compulsory	to finish university
co-educational	must do
degree	qualification from a university
graduate	boys and girls study together

c Finish these sentences.

The school-leaving age in Britain is ...

Pupils go to ... school before secondary school.

There are ... schools for the under-5s.

The national exam at 16 is ...

The national exam at 18 is ...

Universities are part of ...

d i Underline any differences between your system of education and the British system. Write sentences to explain the differences.

ii Draw a diagram to illustrate your education system.

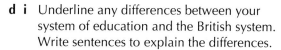

KEY WORDS	**PRIVATE EDUCATION**
independent schools	Seven per cent of British school children go to private schools called **independent schools.** There are 2,400 independent schools and they have been growing in number and popularity since the mid-1980s.
fees boarding school	Parents pay for these schools, and **fees** vary from about £250 a term for a private nursery to £3,000 a term or more for a secondary **boarding school** (pupils board, i.e. live at the school). Most independent schools are called prep schools because they prepare the children for the Common Entrance Exam which they take at the age of 11. This exam is for entry into the best schools.
public schools Eton	The most famous schools are called '**public schools**' and they have a long history and tradition. It is often necessary to put your child's name on a waiting list at birth to be sure he or she gets a place. Children of wealthy or aristocratic families often go to the same public school as their parents and their grandparents. **Eton** is the best known of these schools.
single-sex	The majority of independent secondary schools, including public schools, are **single-sex**, although in recent years girls have been allowed to join the sixth forms of boys' schools. Independent schools also include religious schools (Jewish, Catholic, Muslim etc.) and schools for ethnic minorities.

Reading activity

3 a Find two differences between state and independent schools in Britain.

b Finish these sentences.

The most famous private schools are known as ...

Parents have to pay ... for private schools.

At 11 pupils take the ... to enter public schools.

EDUCATION & TRAINING CHOICES

1 Here are some decisions that British students have to make.

At 16 — stay on at school ? look for a job ? apply for a place on a Youth Training Scheme ?

At 18 — go to university ? get a job ? start a training course ? do voluntary work ? travel and work abroad ? move away from home ?

a Make a list of decisions that students have to make in your education system.

b At 16 ... which choice might Teresa make ? Stay on in the sixth form at school or go to Sixth Form College ?

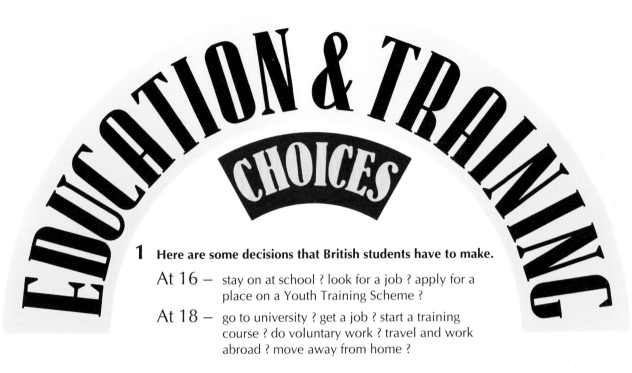

School or College...

Seventeen-year-old Teresa Moore lives in a small village in Wales ...

When I passed my GCSE exams at 16 I decided to continue my studies for two more years. My old school has a small sixth form with about twenty pupils. However, I was not too sure if I wanted to see the same old faces and teachers for another two years. I needed a change!

The Sixth Form College in the nearest city had an open day, and that helped me to decide. I was amazed by the choice of subjects on offer and the canteen and common rooms were very impressive. The pupils seemed so much more grown up, especially as they don't have to wear boring uniforms like in the other place!

On my first day I was sure I had made the wrong decision. The long journey (I have to change bus twice) and the sheer numbers of pupils felt overwhelming, But since then I've settled in, made great new friends and am really enjoying my History, German and English 'A' levels. I couldn't do German at my old school, French was the only language offered. We also do extra Main Studies courses in non-examination subjects – I've chosen photography, journalism and theatre arts – which are really interesting and mean that you get to know lots of people outside your A-level study groups. You can even do rock-climbing or motorcycling!

Reading activity

2 **a** How many subjects does Teresa study?

b Pupils attend a Sixth Form College five days a week from 9am-4pm.
Calculate how many hours Teresa spends on each subject. (Don't forget to subtract seven hours for breaks!)

c Teresa talks about the advantages and disadvantages of going to the college. Tick (✔) the advantages and put a cross (✗) against the disadvantages.

the type of people (not nice) ☐   the facilities ☐
the distance from home ☐   the choice of subjects ☐
the social life (good) ☐   the buildings ☐
the transport ☐   the rules (e.g. clothes) ☐

Pre-reading

3 **At 18 ... Try to predict which of these sentences best describes Chandra's choice:**

a She decided to get a job   **b** She decided to go to university   **c** She decided to get a job before going to university.

FILLING THE GAP...

Eighteen-year-old Chandra Das passed her A-levels in June and has a place at London University to study pharmacy. This year she has chosen not to go straight to London. 'I needed a year out,' she explains.

'The subject I am going to study will lead, hopefully, to a career in industry. But I realised that I didn't know anything about the world at work. I've spent the past six years having a great time in my girls' boarding school but I now need a year of responsibility.

I wrote to a few well-known pharmaceutical companies and one of them offered me a job in their laboratory as a 'work placement'. I'm testing anti-inflammatory drugs at the moment and getting to know more about the technology used in my chosen field. Apart from gaining practical experience, I'm also earning money for the first time in my life! The company are pleased with my work and have offered to sponsor me through university. They will pay me an extra £1,800 a year while I'm studying and I can work in the labs during the holidays.

And at the end of my studies there will be the option of working for them. It has all worked out so well!' says Chandra enthusiastically.

4 **a** Complete this table for Chandra.

Name of university	
Chosen subject	
Present job	
Type of employer	

b Answer TRUE or FALSE.
i Chandra likes earning money.
ii She is still at school.

iii She has got sponsorship for her university course.
iv She went to a private school.

Schools and the world of work

1 **Look at the different activities described opposite.**

    a Does your school organise any of these things?

    b Which subjects in your timetable prepare you for the type of work you want to do?

    c Are there any subjects you would like to add to your school curriculum? Why?

Speaking – group decision-making

2 You are going to plan four visits for pupils in your school next year. These visits are to help pupils apply their studies in a practical way to the 'real' world of work. Which places would you visit? Choose places (companies/offices/industries) in your area which can be linked to the subjects in the table. Try to explain why the visit would be useful.

	PLACE TO VISIT	REASON FOR VISIT
GEOGRAPHY		
MATHEMATICS		
SCIENCE		
CRAFT		

Writing

3 **a** Imagine you are going to spend two weeks working outside your school.
    Where would you like to do your work experience? Give reasons for your choice and describe what you would like to do.

    b Describe the work experience you have had (e.g. holiday/Saturday job). What did you do? Did you enjoy it? Was it useful?

INFORMATION TECHNOLOGY

Most primary and secondary schools in Britain have micro-computers which are used in a wide range of subjects. Experience with information technology helps pupils to acquire the skills needed to work in a modern office or factory.

CAREERS ADVICE

Careers advice is given to pupils in special lessons, particularly in the last years of education. Visitors from different fields of employment come to schools to talk about their jobs and to answer pupils' questions. Pupils also watch TV programmes about jobs. Pupils practise writing job application letters and also hold 'pretend' interviews in class.

SCHOOL OUTINGS

Teachers organise visits to local industry during lesson time. These visits may be to a power station, a factory or an afternoon at a local newspaper office. The visits are often linked to project work for school subjects and pupils write about the visits in class. Sometimes pupils prepare questionnaires and go into the street to interview people for class projects.

WORK EXPERIENCE

Since 1990 all 15-16 year olds are expected to complete two weeks' work experience outside the school in preparation for employment. The school helps pupils to organise suitable placements with local businesses, and pupils share their experiences with their class when they return.

87

Fact File activities

Speaking – group decision-making

1 a Work in groups of six. Imagine that you have to choose a place to study at 16. Put these factors in order of priority from 1 to 8 (1 = most important). Which ones would influence you most in making your decision ?

- friends (Your friends are going to study there.) ☐
- boyfriend/girlfriend (You want to be together.) ☐
- buildings and facilities (modern, new) ☐
- social life (e.g. lots of parties, discos, clubs) ☐
- teachers (friendly and good) ☐
- subjects offered (You like the timetable.) ☐
- the location (You want to live near/away from home.) ☐
- the reputation (People say it is a good school.) ☐

Now discuss your list with the other members of your group. Use this language to help you:

Example:

I think ...   *I think friends are very important. I am not happy at school without my old friends.*

In my opinion ...   *I disagree, it is more important to have good teachers.*

I prefer ...

I like ...

I agree ...

I disagree ...

Try to arrive at a list which reflects the views of your group as a whole.

b Many British students take 'time off' (usually a year) before going into higher education. Here are some examples of what they could do. What would you choose to do ? Tell your group.

work in industry

travel around Europe or the world

work as a volunteer with young people

work on a farm

help with disabled people in local centres or hostels

visit sick people in hospitals

help on a project in Africa

work abroad (washing dishes in restaurants or any job you can find)

work as an *au pair* in Europe or America

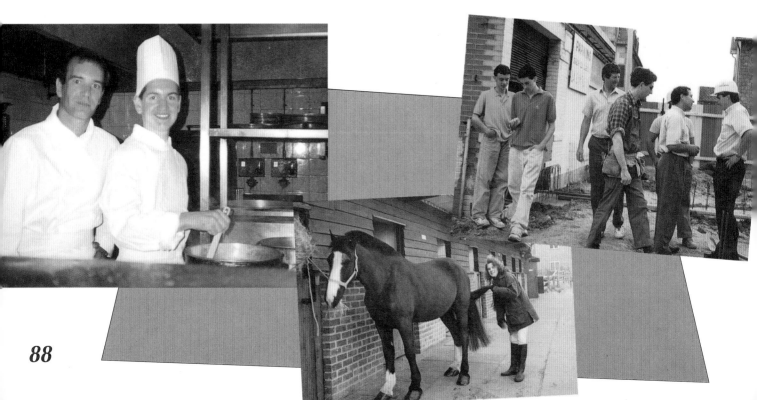

FACT FILE

BRITISH UNIVERSITIES
Did you know ... ?

- There are 97 universities in Britain, including the Open University. 31 former polytechnics were given university status in 1992, as part of a government campaign to increase the number of graduates.

- Students may receive a grant (money) from their Local Education Authority to help pay for books, accommodation, transport and food. This grant depends on parental income.

- Most students live away from home, in shared flats or halls of residence.

- Students don't usually have a job during term time because the lessons, called seminars, classes or tutorials (small groups), are full time. However, many students now have to work in the evenings to supplement their grants.

- Holidays are longer than school holidays – from two to three months in the summer.

- Students do a wide range of summer jobs and holiday jobs at Christmas or Easter.

- Students cannot usually repeat a year. Failing exams is very serious.

- The social life is excellent with a lot of clubs, parties, concerts, bars ...

- Students have their own bank accounts, and banks try to attract students by offering free gifts (presents and money, e.g. typically a cassette tape or pen and £10) at the start of their courses. Banks do this because they think that students are the professionals of the future.

- Most degree courses last 3 years, languages 4 years (including a year spent abroad). Medicine and dentistry courses are longer (5-7 years).

- University life is considered 'an experience'; the exams are competitive but the social life and living away from home are also important.

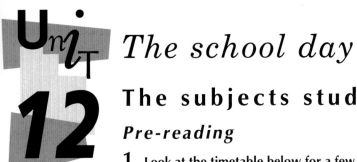

The school day

The subjects studied in a British school

Pre-reading

1 **Look at the timetable below for a few minutes. Now cover the timetable and answer these questions.**

   a How long is an average school day?

   b How often do pupils have breaks?

   c Do pupils start school earlier than in your country?

   d Do you think the lunch break is too short or too long?

   e Do lessons finish later than in your country?

   f Do British children go to school on Saturdays? Do you?

2 **Look at the timetable again. Can you find any subjects which are different from those studied in your school or country?**

	8.45	9-9.15	9.15-10.10	10.20-11.05		11.25-12.20		1.25-2.20	2.20-3.15
MONDAY	Registration	School assembly	Geography	Religious Education	Break	Information Technology	Lunch time	Maths	Science
TUESDAY			French	Art		English		History	Science
WEDNESDAY			PE	PE		Maths		English Literature	Science
THURSDAY			PSE Careers	History		English		CDT	CDT
FRIDAY			Geography	Religious Education		Maths		Performing Arts (music/ drama)	French

KEY WORDS	**DRAMATIC CHANGE – THE NATIONAL CURRICULUM**
Reform	One of the most important changes in education brought about by the **Education Reform Act 1988** is the introduction of a National Curriculum for children aged 5–16 in all state schools in England and Wales. Until the end of the 1980s the choice of subjects to be studied and the content of the lessons were decided by each individual school.
National Curriculum DES syllabus	The **National Curriculum** has changed all of this. The subjects and syllabus are decided by groups of experts working under the **DES** (the Department of Education and Science). Most children in Britain study the same subjects and the same **syllabus**, no matter where they live. It is decided on a national level.
core foundation	The National Curriculum consists of ten subjects which all pupils must study at school. The **core** subjects are English, Mathematics and Science. These are considered the most important because they help you to study all the other subjects. The rest of the subjects are called **foundation** subjects and they include Technology (and design), Music, Art, History, Geography and Physical Education. A modern foreign language, usually French or German, is a foundation subject for all 11–16 year olds.
department	Most schools in Britain divide the subjects and the teachers into **departments**. Each department is responsible for teaching a range of subjects and the teachers in the department have regular meetings to discuss the pupils' work and the syllabus. For example, the Biology, Chemistry and Physics teachers will meet with the Head of the Science Department to plan the work for pupils in that area of study.

Vocabulary work

3 **a** Here is a list of subjects studied in a London comprehensive school. Can you match them to the correct department?

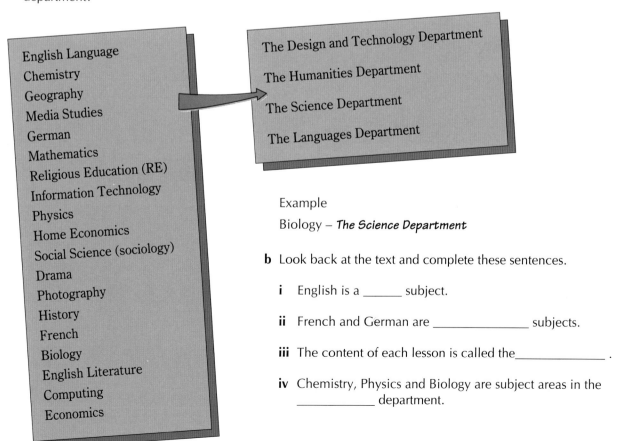

English Language
Chemistry
Geography
Media Studies
German
Mathematics
Religious Education (RE)
Information Technology
Physics
Home Economics
Social Science (sociology)
Drama
Photography
History
French
Biology
English Literature
Computing
Economics

The Design and Technology Department

The Humanities Department

The Science Department

The Languages Department

Example
Biology – *The Science Department*

b Look back at the text and complete these sentences.

i English is a _____ subject.

ii French and German are _____ subjects.

iii The content of each lesson is called the_____ .

iv Chemistry, Physics and Biology are subject areas in the _____ department.

Extra-curricular activities

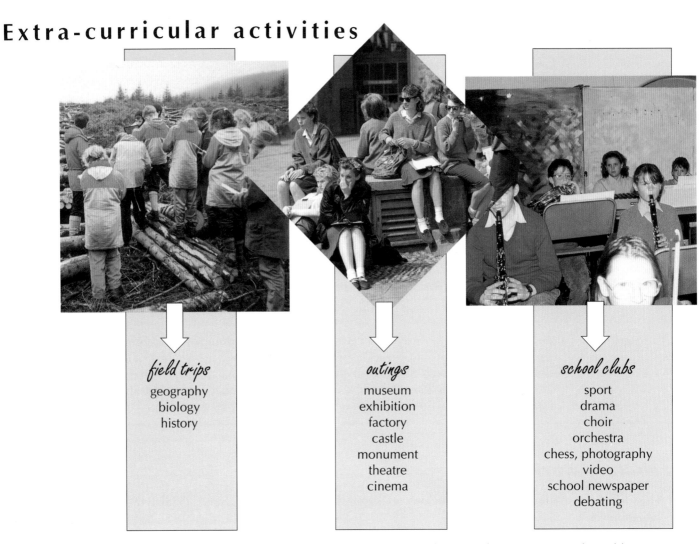

field trips

geography
biology
history

outings

museum
exhibition
factory
castle
monument
theatre
cinema

school clubs

sport
drama
choir
orchestra
chess, photography
video
school newspaper
debating

The activities shown here are called *'extra-curricular activities'* because they are organised in addition to normal school lessons. In British schools, these activities are an important part of learning and of enjoying school.

1 a Tick (✔) any of the activities above which are organised by schools in your country.

  b Make a list of places (monuments/castles/museums) in your own city or area which you would take a group of British students to visit.

2 Interview with a middle-school teacher in the North-east of England

Look at the reporter's note pad. Can you expand his notes into questions? What do you think the answers to the questions will be ? Use the diagram above to help you.

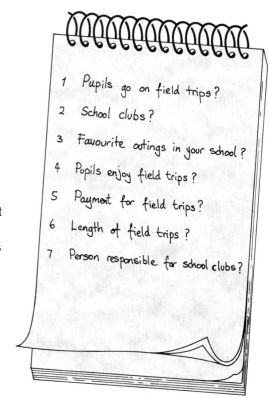

1 Pupils go on field trips?

2 School clubs?

3 Favourite outings in your school?

4 Pupils enjoy field trips?

5 Payment for field trips?

6 Length of field trips?

7 Person responsible for school clubs?

Reading activity

3 Now match the reporter's questions with the correct answers.
Write the number of the question in the space.

Q ....? Yes, they go to hostels in Kielder Forest or to holiday camps like Butlins. They usually go walking, orienteering and canoeing and practise reading maps.

Q ....? Very much. For some pupils it is their first trip away from home and they love sleeping in dormitories. They don't enjoy making meals or washing dishes but that is an important part of the experience !

Q ....? From Monday to Friday. A normal school week.

Q ....? The parents. At one time it used to be the Local Education Authority but recent government cuts have stopped that ! Now we ask parents for a contribution towards the cost, and we try to make the trips as inexpensive as possible.

Q ....? I was teaching 'The Romans' in my history lessons last year so I took the class to the Roman Army Museum – it is always very popular with the kids. They dressed up in replicas of Roman soldiers' uniforms and saw a short film about the Roman Wall (Hadrian's Wall). They also enjoy going to see a play – I try to take them to the theatre once a year.

Q ....? Lots ! There's a video club. They make films when school finishes at four o'clock. They usually write the scripts in their English lessons and perform after school in the hall. The music and drama clubs are particularly active and they have just performed 'Joseph and his Amazing Technicolour Dreamcoat' after many weeks of rehearsals.

Q ....? The teachers, of course. We help and supervise the clubs in our free time. It is a normal part of the job in a British school.

Writing

4 **a** Have you ever been on a school holiday or outing? Describe your experience in no more than 300 words.

or

b Have you ever been away from your parents? Describe where you went, who with, what happened, in no more than 300 words.

The Hidden Curriculum – school discipline

Pre-reading

1 a What is happening in this picture?
Where are they?
Why do you think the boy is being punished?
What type of bad behaviour would you describe as serious?
Does corporal punishment exist in your school?

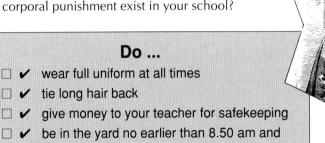

Do ...

- ☐ ✔ wear full uniform at all times
- ☐ ✔ tie long hair back
- ☐ ✔ give money to your teacher for safekeeping
- ☐ ✔ be in the yard no earlier than 8.50 am and no later than 9.00 am
- ☐ ✔ walk
- ☐ ✔ move around school quietly
- ☐ ✔ collect your dinner tickets before 9am
- ☐ ✔ hand your homework in on time

Don't ...

- ☐ ✘ wear mousse, gel or hairspray on your hair
- ☐ ✘ bring jewellery to school
- ☐ ✘ leave money in coat pockets
- ☐ ✘ bring sweets or chewing gum to school
- ☐ ✘ be late
- ☐ ✘ leave your homework until the last minute

b Put a tick (✔) next to the rules which are the same in your school.

c Make a list of Dos and Don'ts in English for your school.

KEY WORDS	ARE SCHOOLS TOO STRICT?
	There are many things which pupils learn in school which are not part of the timetable of official lessons. The term **'hidden curriculum'** is used in Britain to refer to those
hidden curriculum	things pupils learn from the way their school is organised. The school's organisation includes rules, such as punctuality. Pupils are usually expected to arrive at lessons, assemblies and registration on time. Some pupils would say that **school rules** are too
school rules	strict. In the famous progressive boarding school Summerhill, pupils decide what lessons they do and when to do them. In more traditional schools the pupils may be **punished**
punished	for not having a clean school uniform, for failing to wear the school tie or for wearing earrings.
discipline	Teachers are responsible for **discipline** in British schools and they also follow special courses to help them work well with badly-behaved pupils. A pupil is sent to the
Headteacher obedience	**Headteacher** when he has committed a serious offence. The teachers take turns to supervise the corridors and schoolyard during lunch-time. **Obedience** to authority and co-operation with other pupils are important values which teachers communicate to
form tutor	pupils as part of the 'hidden curriculum'. Most pupils also have a **form tutor**; this may be the teacher who is the head of the year group. The form tutor is available to help pupils with their personal problems, give them advice on careers, exams or school reports and is responsible for discipline when the pupil breaks a school rule. Most pupils talk to
PSE	their form tutor in a **PSE** lesson.

Reading activity

2 Complete this diagram with words from the text.

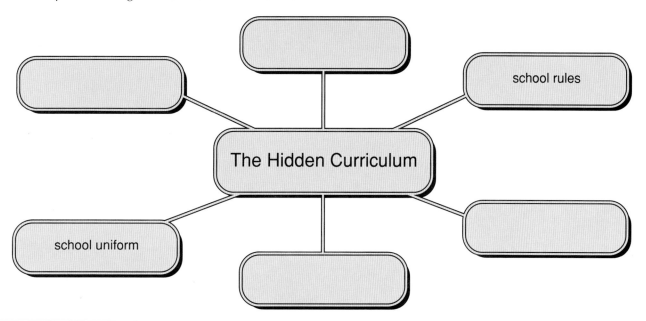

The Hidden Curriculum

school rules

school uniform

KEY WORDS

bullying

the bully

ARE SCHOOLS TOO STRICT?

In recent years, teachers and parents have become more concerned about the problem of **bullying**. Bullying happens when one pupil (or a group) threatens and sometimes physically attacks a younger, weaker, quieter or more timid pupil. This type of behaviour is now considered a serious offence, and articles have been published in the national press about the terrible effects that bullying can have on young people. The victim of bullying can suffer psychologically and the school can suffer too. Persistent bullying of other pupils can lead to **the bully** being excluded. Exclusion is the worst possible punishment in a British school!

Here are some of the punishments in British schools:

Lines: In England, when a teacher gives you 'lines', you write out the same sentence again and again, perhaps fifty or a hundred times. For example, 'I must do my homework,' or 'I must not be late.'

Detention: If you are 'in detention', you stay after school to do extra work - possibly lines - for half an hour or so.

Report: If you are 'on report', you have a card which you give to the teacher at the end of every lesson. Each teacher reports if you have behaved well or badly.

Exclusion: If you are excluded, you cannot come to school for a few days or weeks. Your parents see the headteacher. This is serious.

Expulsion: If you are expelled, you are sent away from your school. This is very serious. You have to go to another school where the teachers all know about your bad record.

Interpretation

3 **a** Who is responsible for discipline in British schools?

b Who do pupils talk to when they have problems with their homework?

c Why is a school bully considered to be dangerous?

d Compare the punishments in British schools with your school. Are they different? Do you think British schools are too strict?

4 Imagine you are a group of teachers in a British school.

    a Look at the list of offences below. Decide if each example of bad behaviour is:
very serious/serious/minor/harmless (= not bad behaviour at all)

          1 running in the corridor

          2 fighting on the floor in the classroom

          3 swearing at a teacher

          4 throwing a piece of paper across the classroom during a lesson

          5 smoking in the school toilets

          6 stealing from other pupils

          7 singing during the lesson

          8 cheating in an exam

          9 looking out of the window when the teacher is giving a lesson

        10 forgetting to bring your homework to the lesson.

    b Now decide with your group which punishment you would give in each of the situations.
For example: Running in the corridor

      *'I think running in the corridor is a minor offence so I would give the pupil lines to write.
He would have to write 100 times "...I must not run ...".'*

Fact File activities

1 Read the Fact File on British schools. Underline any information which is different from your school or schools in your country.

Group work

2 Prepare your own fact file in small groups. It should give information on schools in your country for British teenagers to read.

Pair work

3 Imagine your partner is a pupil at a London school. Interview him/her about a typical school day in London, how the school is organised and what type of subjects he/she studies. Use the Fact File and the timetable on page 90 to prepare your questions. Your partner should use the Fact File to answer your questions.

FACT FILE – A SCHOOL DAY

Did you know that ...

Terms: There are normally three school terms in Britain: Autumn, Spring and Summer terms.

Half-term: The schools usually have five days' holiday halfway through each term. Sometimes schools take their pupils on trips at half-term, e.g. skiing in February or a French exchange visit.

Holidays: This can vary from region to region. The schools usually have ten days at Christmas, ten days at Easter and six weeks in the summer from the end of July to the beginning of September.

School meals: Students can eat lunch in the school canteen. They buy 'dinner tickets' at an inexpensive rate in school. Some students can have 'free school meals' if their parents have a low income. In recent years more and more students have decided to bring their own lunch (sandwiches), known as a 'packed lunch', rather than eat in the canteen. All pupils enjoy discussing how awful school food is.

Schoolyard: In most schools the pupils spend the breaktime and lunch hour in the school yard or on the school field. If the weather is bad they may spend break in the school hall – a very large room for assembly.

School assembly: All schools must by law organise a short daily meeting for the whole school to give important information and give some form of religious worship.

School uniform: Even more popular in recent years. Pupils sometimes wear a blazer and a school cap (more common at private schools than at state schools) or – more usually – a shirt, trousers or skirt, and sweater in the school colours, together with a school tie.

Uni⊤ 13 *British industry*

The Industrial Revolution

Britain has been an industrialised nation for two centuries. It has a variety of industries which can be divided into three main categories.

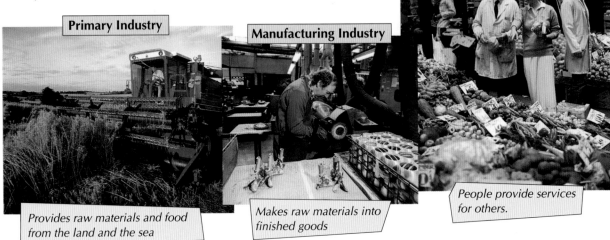

Primary Industry

Provides raw materials and food from the land and the sea

Manufacturing Industry

Makes raw materials into finished goods

Service Industry

People provide services for others.

Pre-reading – Vocabulary

1 a Here are some of the industries in Britain today. Can you match them to the correct category?

> agriculture textiles tourism insurance gas mining transport retail oil food, drink, tobacco fishing business consultancy forestry publishing banking pharmaceuticals cars

Can you think of any other examples?

b Make a list of the main industries in your country.
Make a list of the types of industry in your area.
Who is the biggest employer?
Does anyone in your family work in an industry?

The **coal** and **iron** found in the North-east, the Midlands, Scotland and South Wales provided the power for **factories** in those areas. The **waterways** of Newcastle and Glasgow provided easy access to the sea and **ship-building** industries flourished. **Cotton** arrived at the great port of Liverpool from the USA and India to be made into cloth in the **textile industries** nearby. The sheep in the Yorkshire dales provided wool and the **coalfields** powered the **mills**. The humid climate in Lancashire was particularly good for the **cotton-spinning process**. By 1900 Britain was producing over a third of the world's **manufactured goods** and had earned the title 'The Workshop of the World'.

Read and find out

2 **What was the Industrial Revolution ?**
Why was Britain once called 'The Workshop of the World' ?

BRITAIN'S INDUSTRIAL HERITAGE

During the nineteenth century Britain was transformed from a mainly **agricultural society** into an industrial one. This change has been called the **Industrial Revolution** because of the dramatic effect it had on the British way of life. People moved to the rapidly **expanding towns** and cities, **railways** were developed to transport goods around the country and by 1900 Britain had become a major **world power**.

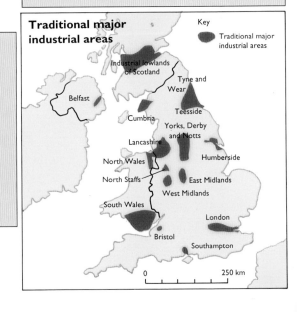

Traditional major industrial areas

Key
Traditional major industrial areas

Industrial lowlands of Scotland
Belfast
Tyne and Wear
Teesside
Cumbria
Yorks, Derby and Notts
Lancashire
Humberside
North Wales
North Staffs
East Midlands
West Midlands
South Wales
London
Bristol
Southampton

0   250 km

Interpretation

3 a The geographical features of Britain had a great influence on Britain's industrial development. Match the features below to the correct industry.

Feature	Industry
The rivers Tyne and Clyde	Textiles (wool) manufacture
The hills and dales of Yorkshire	Mining
The port of Liverpool	Ship building
The coalfields of the North and Wales	Textiles (cotton spinning)

b Heavy industrial development can also have an effect on the surrounding environment. Look for any examples of changes to the way Britain looked. Can you explain why the area around Birmingham became known as the 'Black Country'?

Pre-reading

4 Tick (✔) the sentences which best describe the diagrams.

- ☐ Most people in Britain today work in manufacturing industries.
- ☐ Service industries have dramatically increased since the 1970s.
- ☐ Britain's manufacturing industries were stronger in the 1970s.
- ☐ Service industries employ fewer people today than in the 1970s.

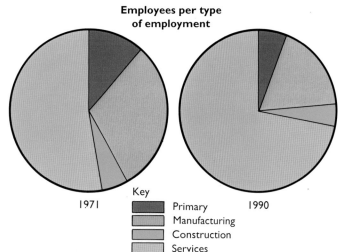

Employees per type of employment

1971   1990

Key
- Primary
- Manufacturing
- Construction
- Services

DECLINE AND CHANGE

The Industrial Revolution in Britain was built on the use of **machines** in factories. Since the 1950s Britain's manufacturing industries have replaced the machine operators with computers and this 'automation' has led to a decline in the number of employees in manufacturing industries. More manufactured goods are bought and used than ever before but a lot of these goods are imported. By the beginning of the twentieth century other industrial countries, like the USA, were competing with Britain's exports and countries in the Far East have been able to provide cheaper products since the 1970s. Areas where **heavy manufacturing industries** are located have suffered high **unemployment**.

During the last 30 years there has been a **rise** in smaller industries, known as **'light industries'**. These industries use **electricity** and are not dependent on raw materials such as coal so they are **'footloose'**, i.e. they can be located anywhere. Many light industries are located on the edge of towns or on industrial estates. They produce such things as washing machines or components. Some of these industries do not make anything at all, but provide **services** such as distribution. The **consumer boom** of the 1980s and the increased leisure time of most Britons has led to rapid growth in **service industries** like banking, tourism, retailing and information-processing, and industries which distribute, maintain and repair household consumer goods.

Comprehension

5 Answer TRUE or FALSE.

a Factories are more automated than they were thirty years ago.

b Light industries have to be located on industrial estates near coalfields.

c Service industries manufacture smaller products.

d Britons buy more consumer goods than thirty years ago.

Writing activity

6 What changes have occurred in your area in the past century ?

- Are towns bigger or smaller ? Are factories bigger or smaller ?
- Do most people do the same jobs as 100 years ago ?
- Write a paragraph describing employment in your area in 1900.
- Write a paragraph describing the main employers and types of work in your area today.

High-tech industries

Pre-reading

1 a Can you name these products which contain a silicon chip? Make a list of other things which use silicon chips.

b Make a list of any electrical or electronic goods in your home. Where were they made?

Read and find out

2 a Why is the British economy influenced by the silicon chip?

b Where is Silicon Valley ?

c Why is Central Scotland called 'Silicon Glen' ?

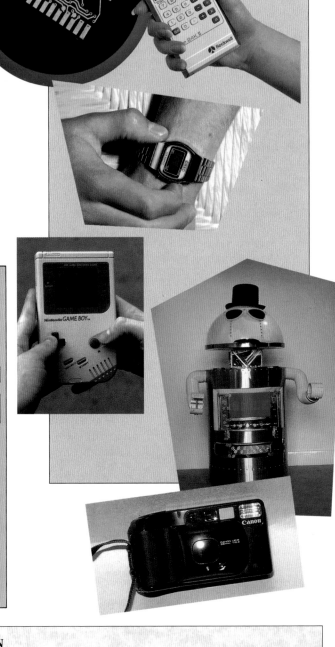

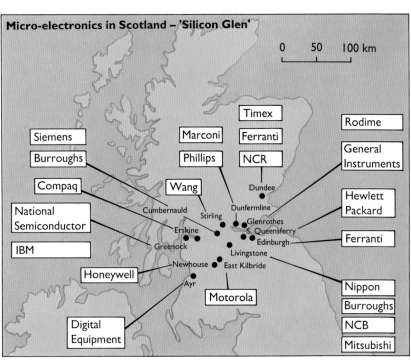

Micro-electronics in Scotland – 'Silicon Glen'

0   50   100 km

Siemens
Burroughs
Compaq
National Semiconductor
IBM
Honeywell
Digital Equipment

Marconi
Phillips
Wang
Timex
Ferranti
NCR

Cumbernauld
Stirling
Erskine
Greenock
Newhouse
Ayr
Dundee
Dunfermline
Glenrothes
S. Queensferry
Edinburgh
Livingstone
East Kilbride
Motorola

Rodime
General Instruments
Hewlett Packard
Ferranti
Nippon
Burroughs
NCB
Mitsubishi

KEY WORDS	THE HIGH-TECH REVOLUTION
electronics industries high-tech	Many Britons own televisions, videos and personal computers. All of these machines are produced by the rapidly-expanding **electronics industries** in Britain. These 'silicon chip' industries are also known as **high-tech** industries and are involved in fields as diverse as aerospace technology, communications and computerised office equipment.
M4 motorway corridor 'Silicon Valley'	The first electronics firms grew up around London and gradually expanded along the **M4 motorway** to the west of the capital, forming a **corridor** of firms known as **'Silicon Valley'**. They were particularly attracted to the area because of the good road links and easy access to London's Heathrow airport. Universities, because of their electronics research, have provided an excellent location for small and large firms. The eight
Scotland 'Silicon Glen' science parks	universities and high percentage of science graduates in **Scotland** have contributed to the concentration of high-tech industries in **'Silicon Glen'**. By 1989 there were 62 **science parks** sited near a university.

Pre-reading

3 **a** Who developed the mass-market pocket calculator?
    b Who are Britain's main competitors in the electronics market?

KEY WORDS

Sinclair
pocket calculator
world's cheapest
  computer

Sir Clive **Sinclair** invented, researched and developed the first cheap **pocket calculators** in the 1970s and established his company, Sinclair Research, in Cambridge to continue his contact with the university there. By 1983 he had developed the **world's cheapest computer** with sound and a colour display and had sold over one million computers worldwide.

inventiveness
research engineers

Sinclair's work is a good example of the **inventiveness** of Britain's electronics industry. Scotland has a reputation for producing high quality **research engineers**. However Britain has been less successful in producing, marketing and selling its electronic goods. There is serious **competition** from goods made in Japan, Hong Kong, Taiwan and other **Far East** countries.

competition
Far East

manual
economy
efficient
unemployment

The government has been providing financial incentives (money) to encourage electronics industries to move to areas with high unemployment. Yet the available workers often come from **manual** jobs and do not have the right skills. The British **economy** is also affected by the high-tech equipment which is making offices and factories so **efficient** that fewer employees are needed, thus adding to the **unemployment** figures. Will micro-electronics provide new jobs or replace jobs with computers ?

Boy playing video games using a Sinclair ZX Spectrum microcomputer

Reading comprehension

4 **Answer** TRUE **or** FALSE.

  a Road and air links are important to electronics firms.
  b Science parks are special universities.
  c Sir Clive Sinclair teaches at Cambridge University.
  d Britain is good at selling its inventions.
  e The electronics industry needs large numbers of
    manual workers.

5 **Compare the map here with the one on page 98.**
Do you notice anything?

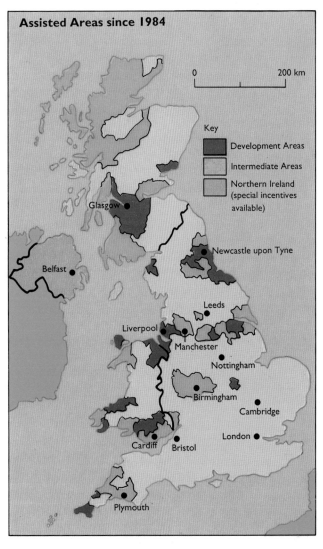

Assisted Areas since 1984

0   200 km

Key

Development Areas

Intermediate Areas

Northern Ireland
(special incentives
available)

Glasgow

Newcastle upon Tyne

Belfast

Leeds

Liverpool
Manchester

Nottingham

Birmingham

Cambridge

Cardiff Bristol

London

Plymouth

The North-South Divide

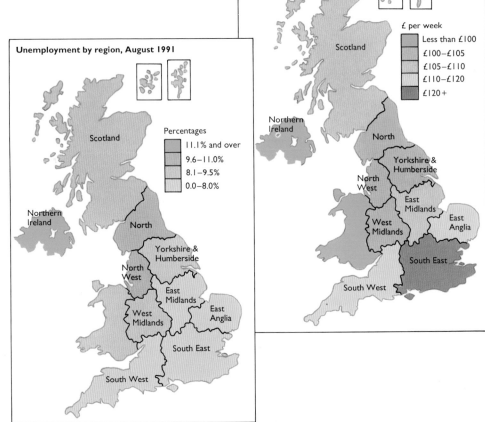

2 Average weekly household disposable income per head, by region 1989

£ per week
Less than £100
£100–£105
£105–£110
£110–£120
£120+

Scotland
Northern Ireland
North
Yorkshire & Humberside
North West
East Midlands
West Midlands
East Anglia
South East
South West

Unemployment by region, August 1991

Percentages
11.1% and over
9.6–11.0%
8.1–9.5%
0.0–8.0%

Scotland
Northern Ireland
North
Yorkshire & Humberside
North West
East Midlands
West Midlands
East Anglia
South East
South West

1

Pre-reading

1 **a** Write two or three sentences comparing the North and South, using the information in the maps.

b List other differences (apart from economic) which may exist between people in the same country, e.g. religion.

Since the 1970s the steady decline of manufacturing industries has led to deserted factories, depressed towns and high unemployment in the areas where they were located. By contrast, the more rural South has experienced the growth of light industries and an increase in clerical and professional jobs. Most of the service industries have developed in southern regions, as well as high-tech firms in the London and Cambridge areas. The increasing affluence of the South during the 1980s contrasted with the problems in the industrial cities of the North and Midlands where school-leavers could not find work and workers were made redundant.

This regional imbalance has been called the North-South Divide and when it was getting worse the word 'gap' was used by the media to explain the great differences in the standard of living of Britons. In the 1980s the government set up 'enterprise zones' in depressed areas and offered companies financial incentives (money/lower taxes) to move to these areas and provide jobs for the unemployed. There was also growing concern that the Channel Tunnel would attract a lot of business and money to the South-east, near its location, whilst the northern areas would not benefit.

At the end of the 1980s the government declared that it had 'solved' the North-South Divide but critics protested that the gap between the regions continued to be a problem. The 1990s economic recession hit the service industries badly, consumers stopped spending, and this had more effect on the affluent South than the North. London, in particular, suffered heavy job losses in retail, financial and banking services. It seemed to be a reversal of the North-South situation. Nevertheless the debate still continues. Are all Britons able to share the same standard of living and job opportunities? How can the traditional industrial areas be assisted? Will the New Europe be closer to the South but too far from the North?

Interpretation

2 **a** The differences between the North and South have been linked to Britain's industrial past. Underline any sentences in the text which mention industrial factors. What other factors have added to this divide? Make a list, using the text and your knowledge of Britain so far.

b Are there any differences between regions in your country? Make a list of the geographical and historical reasons for these variations.

Regional attitudes

Regional differences can also be seen in Britons' views of each other. Most of these attitudes are 'exaggerated' stereotypes and can be unkind. Northerners may be considered 'working class' and 'rough' by some people in the South. Southerners may be considered 'posh' (socially superior) or snobbish (not liking people they think are lower-class) by people living in the northern parts of Britain.

What southerners say about the North	What northerners say about the South
It's dirty and ugly – miles of factories!	They speak with posh accents.
They all live in terraced houses.	They all live in big houses.
They can't speak proper English.	They don't know what 'real work' is.
	They don't care about people less fortunate than themselves.

If you visit Britain you will find that these views are outdated or have *never* been true.
Despite this, you will still occasionally hear such opinions.

Interpretation

3 a Can you suggest any reasons for the attitudes in the table above?
   b Study these photographs of Britain and compare them to the attitudes in the table. Can you find the contradictions?

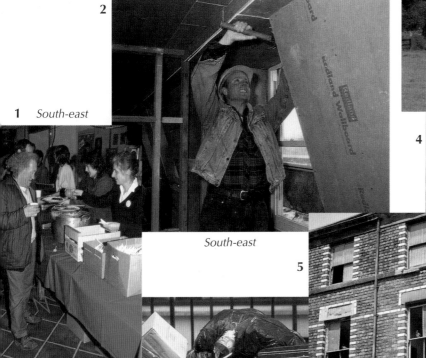

1 *South-east*

South-east

North-east

North-west

South-west

South-east

Discussion

4 a Find two references in the table above to the way people speak.
   b Is accent important in your country?
   c Are some accents or dialects thought to be 'better' than others? Why?

103

Sterotypes

Many people think that this is a typical Englishman.

Some men and some women think that this is a man's job.

Class discussion

Look up the word *stereotype* in a dictionary. What does it mean ?

a National sterotypes are learned from home, friends and the media. For example :

Italians all eat pasta.	The French eat garlic.
The Scottish are mean.	The Irish are stupid.
The English are reserved.	Greeks are passionate.

These generalisations rarely give a true picture as all people are different in each country. Sometimes these sterotypes can be dangerous.

Do people in your country have a sterotyped view of the British ? Are there any national stereotypes ? Do you think they are true or false ?

b Sterotyping in the workplace exists partly because women in the past stayed at home. More and more women work in Britain in a wide variety of jobs and professions. Nevertheless, some Britons (usually men) still believe that there are jobs that women cannot or should not do. Here are some examples from a recent survey in Britain:

Men's jobs: mechanic, bricklayer, manager ...

Women's jobs: nurse, bank clerk, cleaner ...

Do you agree with these opinions ? Are there jobs in your country that women or men traditionally do not do ? Do you think there are jobs that women *should* not do ?

FACT FILE

BRITAIN'S INDUSTRIAL HERITAGE	
British inventions and inventors	1780 The First Industrial Revolution 'The machine age' steam engine civil engineering steam boats electric generator railways mechanised textile manufacture
• The spinning jenny (James Hargreaves 1765) • The steam engine (James Watt 1775) • The turning lathe (John Wilkinson 1778) • The steam locomotive (George Stephenson 1814) • The world's first railway (George Stephenson 1825) • The electric light (Thomas Edison 1879)	1900 The Second Industrial Revolution radio/cinema aeroplanes/motor cars photography/electric motors electrified cities telephone/telegraph oil/rubber/chemical industries
• The first pneumatic tyres (John Dunlop 1888) • Television (John Logie Baird 1926) • The electronic calculator (Alan Turing 1943)	1980 The Third Industrial Revolution 'The computer age' telematics/space probes computers/electronics mass air transport car-based cities plastics/atomic energy artificial intelligence
• The hovercraft (Christopher Cockerell 1953)	1990

The " Rocket."

Trade and Britain's future

Imports and exports

Pre-reading

2	Jamaica
	France
	Spain
	Denmark
	Canada
	India

1 a Match the different sorts of food and drink in the picture to their country of origin.
b How much of the traditional British breakfast comes from other countries ?
c Make a list of the things you eat and drink for breakfast.
d Are any of them imported ? Where from ?

Activity

2 a These British products are world famous. Do you recognise any of them ? Make a table with information about each product. Can you add any more to your list ?

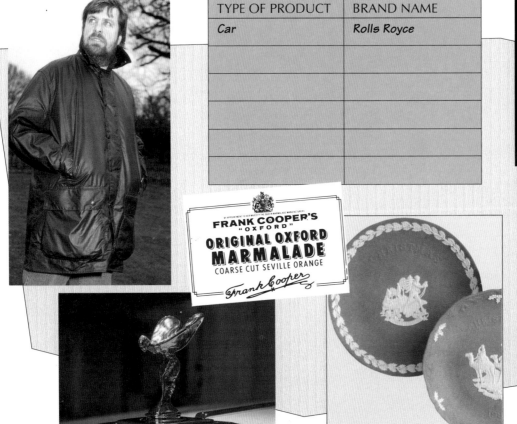

TYPE OF PRODUCT	BRAND NAME
Car	Rolls Royce

FRANK COOPER'S "OXFORD"
ORIGINAL OXFORD MARMALADE
COARSE CUT SEVILLE ORANGE
Frank Cooper

b Have you got anything 'made in Britain' in your home ?

3 Over half of Britain's trade is with the other eleven members of the European Community and this is increasing with the completion of the Single European Market in 1992.

Can you identify the twelve members ? Match the countries/capitals to the map. Is your country a member ?

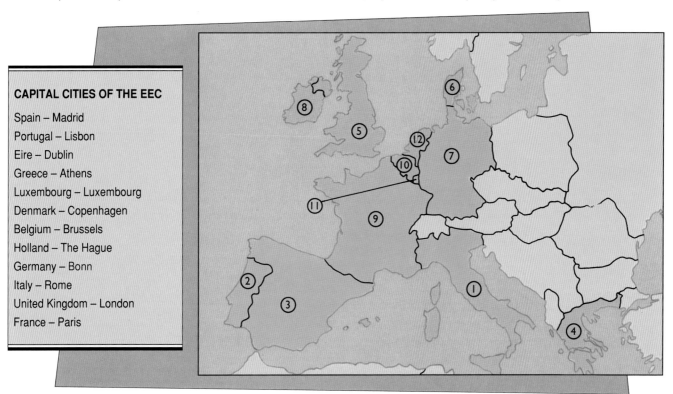

CAPITAL CITIES OF THE EEC

Spain – Madrid
Portugal – Lisbon
Eire – Dublin
Greece – Athens
Luxembourg – Luxembourg
Denmark – Copenhagen
Belgium – Brussels
Holland – The Hague
Germany – Bonn
Italy – Rome
United Kingdom – London
France – Paris

Overseas trade has been very important to Britain's economy for hundreds of years. During the Industrial Revolution Britain developed into an international trading centre. There was so much trade that it had a merchant fleet of ships which was bigger than the rest of the world's put together. Today Britain is the fifth largest trading nation and is part of the world's largest trading bloc, the EEC. In the past, Britain's trade was centred on the Empire and later the countries that made up the Commonwealth. Since joining the EEC and the Single European Act of 1992, Britain has traded less with these old partners because it must use other European suppliers.

Britain's decision to join the EEC in 1973 was mainly for political reasons. Britain wanted to become part of Europe and have more contact with European countries. It was also useful to be a member for economic reasons. Britain is an island and depends a lot on trade with other countries for raw materials and food not found in Britain. The Single European Market offers British companies a market of over 350 million customers. A wide range of goods offering choice to British consumers can also be imported, and the free trade and duty-free arrangements with member countries simplify trade for Britain.

Reading comprehension

4 Use the text to complete this table.

EEC membership since ...	
Main reason for joining	
Other reasons for joining	
Advantages of membership	
Britain's main trading partners	

If your country is a member of the EEC, copy this chart and complete it.

What does the future hold ?

Pre-reading

1 **Read the following texts and answer the questions.**

    a Which text is about ...
        language learning ?
        freight transport ?
        business accommodation ?
        business travel ?

    b Read and find out ...
        the name of London's new airport.
        the name of Britain's new financial district.
        the main language which will be spoken in Europe.
        the main industries where English is used.

①   If you want a share of the highly lucrative London business traveller market, then London City Airport is your best opportunity.

    Within 20 minutes of the business heart of the Capital, it's been specially designed around the business traveller's needs.

    Ready to serve all European points by April 1992, London City Airport offers you the chance to lift your passengers out of the crowd and into a stylish and relaxed V.I.P. environment.

    Now is the time to start your approach.

    Bill Charnock has the details on +44-71-474-5555 (Fax +44-71-473-0356).

LONDON CITY AIRPORT
London's first business airport

② Over the past year, the future role of London Docklands, as a leading new financial and commercial centre within the nation's capital has become increasingly obvious. When the London Docklands Development Corporation was set up in 1981, all but one of the great docks, which had made London one of the world's largest and busiest ports at the beginning of the 1960s, had closed, leaving behind widespread dereliction and massive unemployment. Yet today, in less than a decade, the area is poised to become one of the most significant financial and commercial centres in Europe.

In less than ten years, what was seen by many as an enormous gamble has taken shape as one of the most exciting and ambitious inner-city regeneration projects ever achieved. Though the speed of development will be regulated by ups and downs in the economy, it is now widely recognised that the area has an excellent future – and one which could be critical for the whole of Britain. London is Europe's financial centre – the counterpart of New York and Tokyo – and this was recently underlined by the decision to site the new Bank of European Reconstruction and Development in London. To maintain this position after the creation of the Single European Market in 1992, room must be found not only to meet new European demand, but also to provide the advanced high-tech offices which major international companies now require, and at rents competitive with other European business centres.

③ A NEW EUROPE

Successful business depends on successful communication – for British companies this means being able to use and understand the languages and business culture of our European neighbours.

English may be widely understood in continental Europe, especially in the tourism and leisure industries, but the British companies who really want to exploit the opportunities of 1992 know that they must talk to new customers and new business partners in their own language.

④ The Eurotunnel system will revolutionise freight transport between the UK and mainland Europe. A dedicated HGV shuttle service between Folkestone and Coquelles, near Calais, is designed to provide a round-the-clock service, just turn up any time.

Industry will reap the benefit of meeting "just in time" deadlines.

Faster average journeys, throughout a new Europe without frontiers and crossing problems, will enable hauliers using Eurotunnel to operate more effectively in a competitive market of more than 320 million people.

There will be between two and four shuttle departures per hour in each direction, virtually unaffected by the weather. The combination of speed and convenience will help you to meet your customers' deadlines.

Interpretation

2 Britain's future depends on European trade. In the late 1980s and early 1990s a number of things were done to prepare for 1992. At the same time there were a lot of important precautions to be taken. Use the texts to make notes on :

a What the British have done to prepare themselves
b What should be done/needs to be done in the 1990s to ensure that Britain benefits from the Single Market.

Pre-reading

3 Look at this map and at the headline and diagram from *The Sunday Times.*

a What do you think each article is about ?
b What do you think 'Euro-talent' means ?
c What exactly does a 'head-hunter' do in the world of employment ?
d Why do you think people would choose to live and work abroad ?
e What things, apart from goods, do British companies want to trade ?

Source: *Sunday Times*, 28 May 1989

As 1992 and a single European market loom ever closer, Marks & Spencer's recruiters have taken the step across the Channel to shop for top Continental graduates. Jane Fisher investigates.

Reproduced by permission of Marks & Spencer plc

Read and find out

4 **a** Why did Philippe decide to leave France ?
b Why has Alicia chosen Marks & Spencer for her placement year ?
c Would you like to live abroad ? Where would you choose to live and work ?

Alicia Garcia Lopez is a 21-year-old business studies student at the Universidad Pontificia de Comillas in Madrid. She is sponsored by the EEC to spend two years of her four-year course in companies abroad. She has already spent a year in France. She is studying part-time at The Middlesex Business School in London and is working on a student placement at Marks & Spencer. "I spent three summers in Ireland and England, the first when I was eleven. It's a great experience living abroad. I've learnt so much just from living and working here – sorting out problems with the landlord for example !"

Philippe Sauce is a 25-year-old French accountant. He has recently been recruited by M&S as part of their foreign graduate recruitment scheme. He is currently training in London. Why did he choose to work in another country ?

"It's very important for me to work abroad. It makes my career more interesting, from a personal point of view. I want to meet new people in new countries and learn new languages. This company is offering me training and opportunities that will help me move forward into management."

109

Made in Britain?

Pre-reading

1 Look at the names of the companies in the box and answer the questions.

  a Where are they from?
  b What do they produce?
  c What do you know about these companies?
  d Have you got any of their products in your country/home?

TOYOTA	SONY
HONDA	NISSAN
TOSHIBA	MITSUBISHI
NINTENDO	SANYO

2 Read and find out:

  a Where is Sunderland?
  b Which company has set up a factory in Sunderland?
  c Is it the only Japanese company in Britain?

THE SUCCESS STORY

In 1984 470 jobs were advertised in Sunderland, an industrial city in the North-east of England. 25,000 people applied for those jobs. This traditional manufacturing area was suffering from the worst unemployment rate in the country. Anxious to solve the problems of depressed areas, the British government tried to attract new companies to these places with special financial incentives.

Nissan, a Japanese car manufacturer, responded swiftly to the British need. The original 470 jobs rose to over 3,500 by 1992 and the region was given an economic boost. The Sunderland manufacturing plant was built in a record 62 weeks and by 1992 the exports from Sunderland had made a significant contribution to the British balance of trade, since 80% of production is exported. In addition, Nissan offered contracts to 179 European manufacturers and visitors to the Sunderland plant were impressed by the efficient Japanese-style methods of working. British newspapers in 1992 carried news of the success story of Sunderland, and of the numerous other Far Eastern companies which had chosen Britain for their European operations. However, not everyone saw this as a success story ...

Reading comprehension

3 a Use the text to complete this table with notes.

The advantages for Britain	The advantages for Sunderland

    b What do you think are the possible advantages for Nissan?

Pre-reading

4 Not everyone saw the presence of Far Eastern companies in Britain as a positive move. Who do you think might have disagreed? Why? Then read and find out the answer.

Engine plant, Nissan Sunderland

THE TROJAN HORSE

European manufacturers have faced heavy competition from Far Eastern companies since the 1970s. The Japanese in particular were, and still are, viewed as a threat to the European economy since they produce cheaper, high-quality products. For this reason, restrictions were imposed on the number of products that these companies could import into Europe, in order to protect European manufacturers.

However, the cars made in Sunderland are built by British workers, using European components, and are therefore recognised as British products. Far from applauding the success story, some European manufacturers look upon Britain as the Japanese 'Trojan Horse'. These products can be distributed freely within the EEC because they are considered British. Naturally, Britain has given these Far Eastern companies a greater chance of selling in Europe but, for Britain, their presence has been a vital and much-needed boost to the economy. It is a success story with two outcomes!

Reading comprehension

5 **Read and answer.**

   a Give two reasons why Nissan cars are considered British.

   b Give two reasons why European manufacturers think the Japanese companies in Britain are a threat.

Discussion

6 During the 1980s Britain had a public information campaign to persuade the British public to 'Buy British'. The idea behind this was to encourage people to support their country's industries by spending money on locally produced goods.

Which of these factors would you consider important in buying, for example, a car? Put them in order of importance (1-7).

- ☐ the design (I like the 'look'.)
- ☐ the manufacturer (It was made in my country.)
- ☐ the size (It is right for my family and my needs.)
- ☐ the price (It is very reasonable.)
- ☐ the quality (It is reliable.)
- ☐ personal recommendation (I know someone who has one and they say it is very good.)
- ☐ fashion (This type is very fashionable at the moment.)

Final assembly, Nissan Sunderland

FACT FILE ACTIVITIES

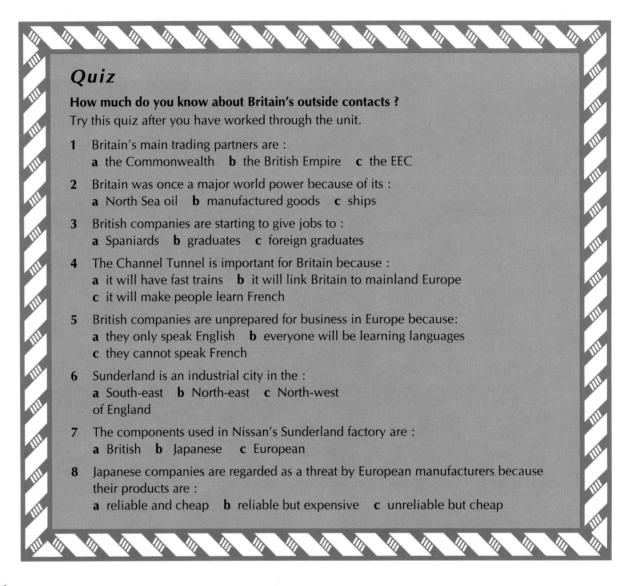

Quiz

How much do you know about Britain's outside contacts ?
Try this quiz after you have worked through the unit.

1 Britain's main trading partners are :
   a the Commonwealth   **b** the British Empire   **c** the EEC

2 Britain was once a major world power because of its :
   a North Sea oil   **b** manufactured goods   **c** ships

3 British companies are starting to give jobs to :
   a Spaniards   **b** graduates   **c** foreign graduates

4 The Channel Tunnel is important for Britain because :
   a it will have fast trains   **b** it will link Britain to mainland Europe
   c it will make people learn French

5 British companies are unprepared for business in Europe because:
   a they only speak English   **b** everyone will be learning languages
   c they cannot speak French

6 Sunderland is an industrial city in the :
   a South-east   **b** North-east   **c** North-west
   of England

7 The components used in Nissan's Sunderland factory are :
   a British   **b** Japanese   **c** European

8 Japanese companies are regarded as a threat by European manufacturers because
   their products are :
   a reliable and cheap   **b** reliable but expensive   **c** unreliable but cheap

---

1 Look at the diagrams opposite and answer the questions.

   a Can you explain the difference between visible and invisible trade ?
   b Which two countries does Britain sell to the most ?
   c Which two countries does Britain buy from the most ?
   d How many of the trading partners in the two pie charts are EEC countries ?
   e What makes up the highest proportion of Britain's exports ?
   f What makes up the highest proportion of Britain's imports ?
   g Who are your country's main trading partners ?
   h Study the contents of your bag. What percentage of the things in it were made in your country ?

Project work

2 a Find out about companies in your area: where do they export to ? Do they have any contact with Britain ?
   Who are their customers abroad ?

   b Collect information on British goods to be found in your country. Find out from your local Chamber of
   Commerce as much as you can about your country's contacts with Britain.

FACT FILE

Examples of Britain's invisible export trade

1a

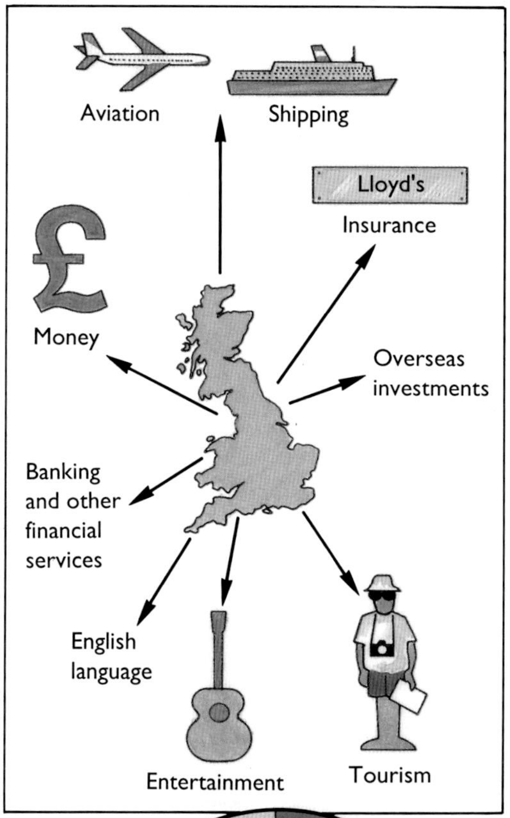

- Aviation
- Shipping
- Lloyd's — Insurance
- Money
- Overseas investments
- Banking and other financial services
- English language
- Entertainment
- Tourism

Examples of Britain's visible trade

1b

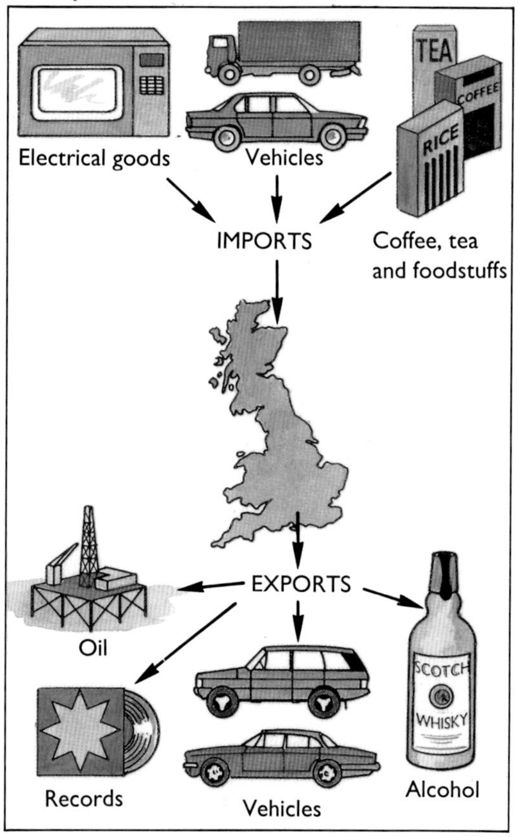

- Electrical goods
- Vehicles
- Coffee, tea and foodstuffs

IMPORTS

EXPORTS

- Oil
- Records
- Vehicles
- Alcohol (SCOTCH WHISKY)

3a

Britain's main markets

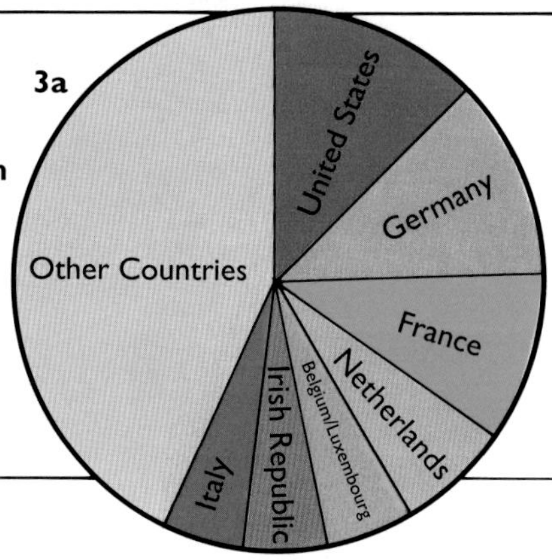

- Other Countries
- United States
- Germany
- France
- Netherlands
- Belgium/Luxembourg
- Irish Republic
- Italy

Britain's main suppliers

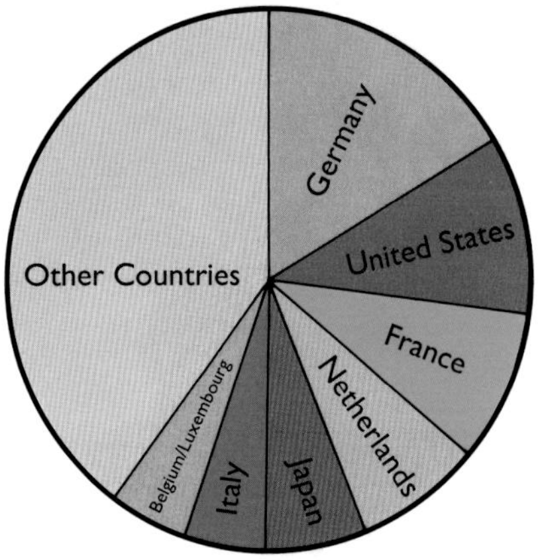

- Other Countries
- Germany
- United States
- France
- Netherlands
- Japan
- Italy
- Belgium/Luxembourg

Britain's balance of trade

2

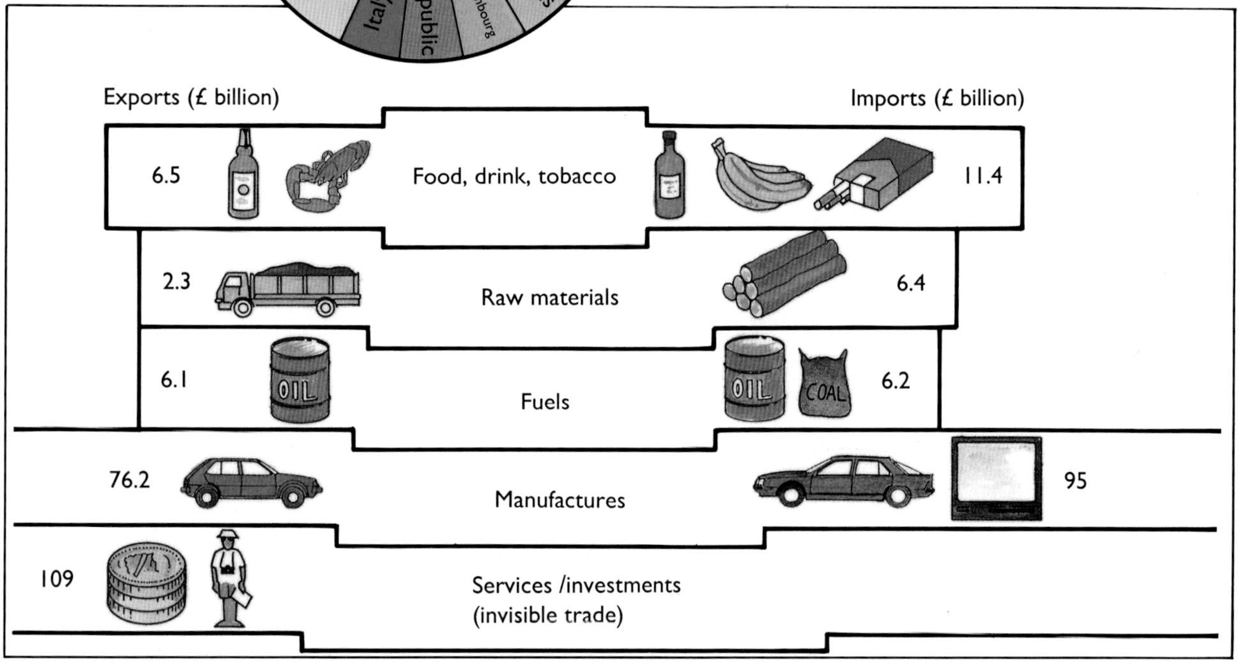

Exports (£ billion)		Imports (£ billion)
6.5	Food, drink, tobacco	11.4
2.3	Raw materials	6.4
6.1	Fuels	6.2
76.2	Manufactures	95
109	Services /investments (invisible trade)	

The high street revolution

The unit of currency is the **pound sterling**. One pound is divided into 100 new **pence** (p). There are **seven** coins. The Bank of England issues banknotes and Scotland has its own banknotes.

decimal point

£2.50

pounds — pence

Two pounds, fifty (pence)

Pre-reading

1 Study the diagram above and answer these questions.

   a *What's the total ?*

      i   £2.00 + 50p + 25p = ...

      ii £5.00 – £1.75 = ...

      iii 20p + 99p + 23p = ...

   b *Write out the amounts in words.*

      i   £6.00

      ii £6.99

      iii 60p

2 **a** Write the exchange rate against the pound sterling in your currency: £1 = ...

   b Write these prices in your currency (prices based on 1992 figures).

Prices (typical)	Your Currency
The average chocolate bar costs 35p.	
A video cassette costs £3.99.	
A compact disc costs £12.99.	
A daily newspaper costs 45p.	
A loaf of bread costs 70p.	

114

3 Compare the British prices with prices for similar items in your country. Are some things cheaper or more expensive ?

KEY WORDS	DECIMAL AND METRIC
decimal new system	In 1971 Britain changed to **decimal** currency. Many young people in Britain today do not remember the old money. The change caused confusion in the first months, so shops showed both old and new money prices to help customers. Schools taught their pupils new maths to cope with the **new system**.
metric feet and inches	Britain also changed to a **metric** system of measurement in the 1970s, but people continue to use the traditional British system of **feet and inches**. People will usually give you their height, weight and even shoe size using the old system. Most clothing manufacturers put both types of measurement on labels.
pounds kilos gallons and litres miles kilometres	In shops the old weights and measures still persist and people may ask for their fruit and vegetables in **pounds** rather than **kilos**. Petrol stations show you the price of petrol in **gallons and litres**. People travel **miles** or **kilometres**. As you can imagine, a conversion table and a pocket calculator are very useful if you visit Britain. Don't forget them, unless you are a mathematical genius !

Interpretation

4 **Use the conversion tables to answer these questions.**

   a If you want to buy tomatoes in a shop you can say :
     I'll have 11 pounds, please, or *I'll have .... kilos*
     How many kilos ?

   b If someone says *I'm five feet, two inches*, how tall is she in metres ?

   c It's 658 kilometres from London to Edinburgh. How many miles ?

5 Imagine you have to tell a British person this information about yourself. Complete the chart using the pre-metric system.

Personal Information	Numbers	Words
Weight		
Height		
Distance from home to school		
Price of petrol in your country		

Speaking

6 Ask and answer questions using the conversion table:

   How much/How far/How tall ... ?

CONVERSION TABLES

Length
1 centimetre = 0.394 inches
1 metre = 39.4 inches
1 metre = 3.28 feet
1 metre = 1.09 yards
1 kilometre = 0.621 miles

Weight
1 gram = 0.035 ounces
1 kilogram = 2.2 pounds
1 metric tonne = 2200 pounds
1 metric tonne = 0.984 tons

Capacity
1 millilitre = 0.035 fl. ounces
1 litre = 1.76 pints
1 litre = 0.22 UK gallons
1 US gallon = 0.833 UK gallons

Area
1 sq cm = 0.155 sq inches
1 sq metre = 10.76 sq feet
1 sq metre = 1.2 sq yards
1 hectare = 2.47 acres
1 sq km = 247 acres
1 sq km = 0.386 sq miles

Volume
1 cu cm = 0.061 cu inches
1 cu metre = 35.3 cu feet
1 cu metre = 1.31 cu yards

A nation of shoppers

Pre-reading

1 **Study the pictures below and answer the questions. Which type of shop do you think ...**

a offers the best choice of goods ?

b has lower prices ?

c gives the best service ?

d is more convenient ?

Which type of shop would you prefer to shop at ?

An out-of-town superstore

A corner shop

The Demise of the Corner Shop

Napoleon Bonaparte once described Britain as 'a nation of shopkeepers', but since the 1960s the traditional corner shop has been slowly disappearing. The neighbourhood corner shop used to sell everything a housewife needed and the shopkeeper was an important person in the local community. The shop itself was a focus of community life, a place to chat as well as shop, in the days when Britons knew their local baker, local grocer and local butcher personally. So what happened to the corner shop ?

Shopping patterns changed dramatically in the 1970s and 1980s and the customers changed too. This change has been called the 'High Street Revolution'. Shops began to get bigger and the owners opened more branches in different towns, each branch selling the same goods and offering cheaper prices than the local corner shop. The smaller shops closed as these large 'chains' of shops took over. Customers liked the chains as they were self-service, offered a wider range of goods and introduced credit cards for customers. People in Britain now like shopping at a 'name' they know, because they can be sure of the quality.

The very large retailers have such an enormous number of stores that they are called multiple retailers. During the 'economic boom' of the 1980s the multiples developed superstores, offering an even wider choice of goods at even cheaper prices, on the edge of towns where giant shopping complexes often grew up around them.

Now that most Britons are car-owners they are prepared to travel further to shop, and like the choice offered by big stores. Most people are now paid monthly and prefer to buy in bulk (large quantities) once a month. The self-service and late-night shopping at superstores is convenient for the many women who work during the week. The corner shop is now empty during the day and people tend to use their local shops only in emergencies, if they have 'forgotten' to buy something.

Corner shops are no longer profitable in the face of competition from the 'giants'. Britain could now be described as a nation of multiple retailers (some with over 200 stores nationwide). Who could hope to survive and compete against their computerised distribution systems, enormous choice and cheap prices ? Supporters of the corner shop say they prefer to pay higher prices because they get a friendlier and more personal service. Others shop there because they have no choice – the elderly or disabled, people without cars and young mothers with small children for whom a trip to a superstore would take a lot of planning and effort – but they are in the minority. Unfortunately for small shopkeepers, the majority of customers prefer speed and choice to the personal service of their local shop.

Reading activity

2 **a** Give two reasons why Britons prefer to shop at large retailers.
   b What is the difference between a shopkeeper and a multiple retailer ?
   c Who shops at corner shops nowadays ?
   d Are there a lot of corner shops in your area/country ?

Writing

3 Write a short paragraph comparing corner or small shops with multiple retailers. Use the following adjectives to help you:

> convenient   cheap
> expensive   friendly
> fast   profitable

The Gateshead MetroCentre – Europe's largest
out-of-town covered shopping centre

Vocabulary

4 **Try this 'Shopping in Britain' puzzle and find the name of Britain's largest retailer.**

Clues

1 Shopping in Britain is in the hands of a few ...
2 A person who runs a small shop is called a ...
3 Some shops have a ... in every high street.
4 Superstores can offer a much wider ... of goods.
5 Shops where you can choose the goods by yourself are ...
6 Very large supermarkets are also called ...
7 A number of shops all owned by the same company are called ...
8 ... shops cannot compete with large retailers.

Retail technology

Pre-reading

1 **a** When you shop in Britain today, your till receipt contains a lot of information. Study the store receipt here and label the information. The first one has been done for you.

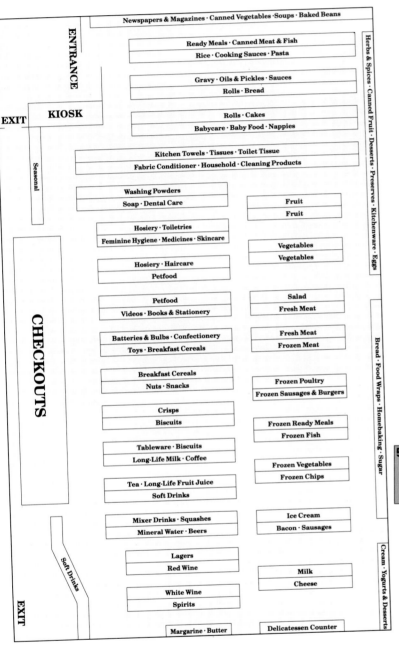

b **i** Try to match as many items as possible on the till receipt to the area of the store where they are displayed.

ii Superstores sell a lot more than food. What other types of goods can you find on the floor plan? Make a list.

How much choice is there in supermarkets in your country? Are there any superstores like Tesco or Sainsbury?

Read and find out

2 a Look at the picture of the girl working at the checkout. The equipment she is using has revolutionised shopping in Britain and all large retailers now use it. Read and label the picture with the words in the box.

display panel   bar code   till
till receipt   cashier   scanner

A NEW WAY TO CHECKOUT AT TESCO

HOW THE SCANNING SYSTEM WORKS

With the introduction of Scanning at Tesco, the cashier will no longer ring-up the price on a cash register.

From now on nearly all the items will be passed over an electronic Scanner that 'reads' the product description, size and price from the information included in the bar code.

All this information is then accurately displayed for both you and the cashier to see on the customer display panel and also printed on your till receipt. For any product which does not carry a bar code, it will be priced and rung up as before.

All prices will continue to be shown on the shelf edge of all displays in the usual way.

When an item is reduced in price the cashier will ring up the lower price and then scan the item. The scanning system will then charge the lower price.

For fresh produce such as loose fruit and vegetables, there will no longer be a produce weigh-and-price point. From now on, these items will be weighed and priced using the scales at each checkout. All fresh produce sold in this way will be described fully on your till receipt with the weight, price per pound and total price.

After paying for your goods, you will be given a till

receipt which itemises each product bought, the price, the method of payment, any coupons used, the amount paid, your change, the checkout number, time of day and date.

While Scanning is a useful method of stock control for us, the greatest benefit by far is that it is a fast, accurate system which makes paying for your goods at the checkout much easier. Which all goes to make shopping at Tesco even more of a pleasure than ever.

b Put these sentences in the correct order and draw a diagram to show how EPOS (Electronic Point of Sale = Scanning) works.

- A   The price is relayed automatically back to the checkout.
- B   The cashier runs the bar code over a laser scanner.
- C   The computer automatically "looks up" the price for the product.
- D   A description of the product and its price appear on the display panel.
- E   The information is relayed to a central computer data store.
- F   A description of the product and its price appear on the customer's till receipt.

c Make a list of the possible advantages of EPOS for customers and for retailers.

A High Street Name

1882   A Russian refugee, Michael Marks, began selling haberdashery in villages in the North-east of England.

1884   Marks saved enough money to set up a market stall in Leeds and placed a sign on his stall which read 'Don't ask the price – it's a penny'.

1894   Marks had eight market stalls and invited Tom Spencer to be his business partner.

1926   Marks & Spencer had 126 branches throughout Britain and had become a public limited company.

1992   The company had over 685 stores worldwide. Millions of Britons shop every week at M & S for clothes or food. Marks & Spencer is one of the most admired companies in Britain today and has a reputation for high-quality goods at moderate prices. Unfortunately, you cannot buy anything for just a penny now!

FACT FILE

Opening and closing times

Post offices	Shops
• 9am – 5.30pm (Mon-Fri) 9am – 12.30pm (Sat) • Some London post offices are open 8am-8pm	• 9am – 5.30 (Mon-Sat) • Late-night shopping on Thursdays until 8pm • Half-day closing on Wednesday (some towns)
Banks	**Supermarkets/superstores**
• 9.30am – 3.30pm (Mon-Fri) 9.30am – 12.30pm (Sat)	• 9am – 8pm (Mon-Sat) • Late-night shopping on Friday until 9pm • Many supermarkets now open on Sundays (restricted hours, typically 10am – 4pm) and most open on public holidays.

Sunday trading

Shopping hours in Britain are controlled by law (1950 Shops Act). Certain goods cannot be sold on Sundays, but this applies only to England and Wales. Some retailers are open late in the week and corner shops stay open late even although it is against the law.

Many high streets are deserted on Sundays. The Church is generally against Sunday trading because Sunday is a 'day of rest'. Some employers maintain that Sunday opening would create more jobs, thus easing the unemployment problem. Other people argue that shop workers might be compelled to work on Sundays against their will because they would risk losing their jobs if they refused. The national press and the government have been debating this question for over thirty years. However, the Sunday trading laws are now so widely disregarded that a change in the law seems inevitable.

What can you buy on Sundays in your country ? Do you think people should be allowed to shop on Sundays ?

Consumer credit

- Has increased substantially since 1981; consumer debt trebled in the 1980s.
- A very high proportion of household expenditure is financed through credit cards. In the 1980s many Britons spent more than they earned.
- In 1975 3.3 million people had Visa cards; by 1988, 15.3 million people had a Visa card.
- Two-thirds of all adults in Britain have some form of 'plastic money' card.
- Shops introduced interest-free credit in the 1980s. This encouraged heavy spending.

Acknowledgements

The author and publishers wish to thank the following who have kindly given permission for the use of copyright material:

British Broadcasting Corporation for programme content from *Radio Times* issue of 3-10 October 1992;

British Railways Board for route map and information from *Intercity* pamphlet;

BUAV for their 'Paradise Lost' advertising poster;

The Channel Tunnel Group Ltd for extracts from their promotional material;

Docklands Light Railways Ltd for material from their promotional brochures;

EMAP Apex Publications Ltd for the front cover of *Practical Gardening*;

EMAP Elan for the front cover of *Slimming* magazine;

EMAP Metro for the front cover of *Q* magazine;

Evening Chronicle (Newcastle upon Tyne) for material from their 25.5.91 and 2.7.91 issues;

Gordon Fraser Gallery for card 'A New Home' by Kate Veale, UH1;

Greenpeace for advertising material;

Guardian News Service Ltd for material from their 1.2.91 and 22.10.92 *Guardian* issues:

Hanson White-Accord for card 'Sorry You're Leaving';

Health Education Authority for material from 'Guide to Sensible Drinking', 'That's the Limit' and 'A Guide to Sensible Eating';

IPC Magazines Ltd and the Antique Collectors Club for front cover of *Country Life*;

IPC South Bank Publishing Group for letter in *Mizz*, 19.2.91, on page 57

The Controller of Her Majesty's Stationery Office for material from *Social Trends*, 1991, 1992, and *Britain 1992: an Official Handbook*;

House of Commons for material from 'Parliament and Government', Education Sheet 1;

League Against Cruel Sports for advertising material;

Lloyds Bank Plc for the front cover of 'Lloyds Bank Fashion Challenge' leaflet, 1992;

London City Airport for advertising material;

London Docklands Development Corporation for an extract from their Annual Report;

London Transport Museum for material from their promotional pamphlets and the London Underground map;

London Underground Ltd for material from their promotional material and ticket;

Marks & Spencer plc for material from 'Marks & Spencer's World';

The National Magazine Company Ltd for the front cover of *Good Housekeeping* and material from 'The Best of British', *Company*, Nov., 1990;

Thomas Nelson and Sons Ltd for material from *Communication and Media Studies*, Macmillan; *The British Isles*, 2nd edition, by David Waugh; and *The Industrial Age: Questioning History 4*;

Newspaper Publishing PLC for 'BR will take you closer' by Trevor Barnes, *Independent*, 4.7.91; 'Young Voices, Old Problems' and two graphics, *Independent on Sunday*, 4.8.91; and material from *Independent*, 31.1.91;

The Open University, for an adaptation from *Sociology in Practice*, E354 Block 3 Unit 10;

Oxfam for snowman card design;

Pitman Publishing for material from *Franc Exchange*, published for the BBC;

Redwood Publishing Ltd for the front cover of *Clothes Show* magazine;

J. Sainsbury plc for table from 'Sensible Drinking', Living Today leaflet No.5;

Simon and Schuster Young Books for 'A New Life in Britain' from *People Then and Now*;

Jean Stern for 'Help your kids to spend wisely', *Best*, 30.5.91;

Times Newspapers Ltd for illustration 'Where the workers are going' and headline 'Hunt for Eurotalent won't be all one way', *Sunday Times*, 28.5.89;

World Wide Fund for Nature UK for 'What On Earth Can I Do' logo;

Joseph Wright for cartoon, *Best*, 30.5.91.

Every effort has been made to trace all the copyright holders but if any have been inadvertently overlooked the publishers will be pleased to make the necessary arrangement at the first opportunity.

The author and publishers acknowledge with thanks the following photographic sources for the use of copyright material:

BBC p79; Channel Tunnel Group Ltd p40; Dialogue pp 87, 88; DP Photographic p14; Greg Evans pp2, 3, 10, 20, 23, 24, 26, 28, 30, 36, 38, 50, 51, 56, 61, 62, 68, 71, 80, 83, 84, 85, 87, 89, 92, 96, 97, 98, 100, 103, 104, 106, 116, 120, 121; Mary Evans Picture Library pp3, 6, 94, 105; Sally and Richard Greenhill pp6, 8, 89, 104; Clare Lavery pp89, 90, 92, 95; Marks & Spencer PLC p120; Nissan Motor Manufacturing UK Ltd pp110, 111; Popperfoto Ltd pp74, 80; Rex Features pp2, 3, 12, 14, 20, 23, 24, 30, 36, 38, 41, 45, 50, 51, 53, 61, 62, 74, 80, 81, 100; Chris Ridgers pp30, 103, 106, 114; Science Photo Library pp20, 100, 101, 105; Telegraph Colour Library p100; Trident pp87, 88; Zefa pp20, 56, 58, 61, 89